Corfu
and Mainland
Greece
2nd Edition

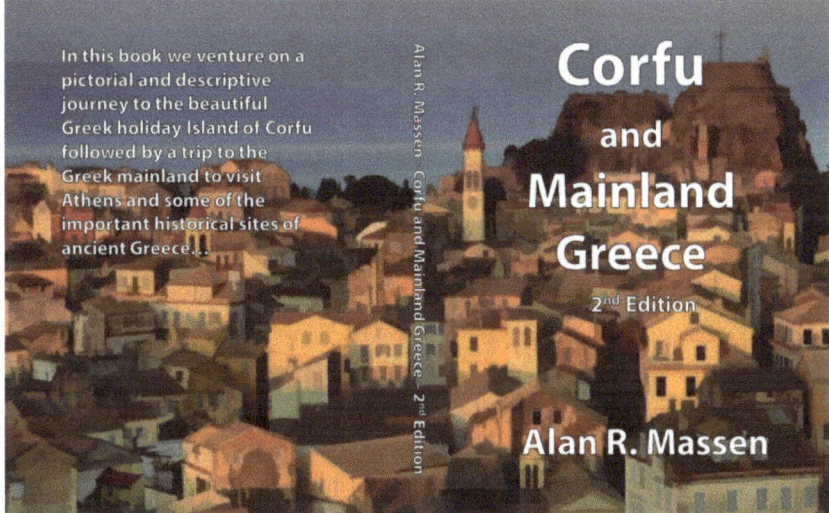

Corfu and Mainland Greece is a pictorial and descriptive journey through the history and beauty of the Greek paradise Island of Corfu before we sail away on a trip to the mainland of Greece to visit some of the most important historical sites of ancient Greece.

by Norfolk Watercolour Artist - Alan R. Massen
Published in Great Britain by Rainbow Publications UK

First Published in 2018 by Rainbow Publications UK
2nd Edition Published in 2019 by Rainbow Publications UK

Copyright © 2019 Alan R. Massen

The moral right of Alan R. Massen to be identified as the author of this work has been asserted in accordance with the UK Copyright, Designs and Patents Act of 1988. All rights reserved.

No part of this book may be reproduced, or stored in a retrieval system, or transmitted in any form or by any means, electronic, mechanical, photocopying, recording, or otherwise, without the prior written permission of both the author and the above publisher of this book All imagery and illustrations

© Alan R. Massen

Neither the publisher nor the author can accept liability for the use of any of the materials, methods or information recommended in this book or for any consequences arising out of their use, nor can they be held responsible for any errors or omissions that may be found in the text or may occur at a future date as a result of changes in rules, laws or equipment All manufacturers, sellers, product names and services identified in this book are used in editorial fashion and for the benefit of such companies with no intention of any infringement of trademarks. No such use or the use of any trade name is intended to convey endorsement or other affiliation with this book

Paperback Edition ISBN 978-0-9935591-5-0
Typeset in Minion Pro
Published in Great Britain by Rainbow Publications UK

About the Author

Alan was born in the city of Norwich in the county of Norfolk, England in November 1949. When Alan was still a teenager he started painting whilst attending art classes in Norwich. In his mid-teens he had two paintings accepted for a National Art Exhibition held in London and other major UK cities. Alan spent most of his working life as a professional Health and Safety Advisor and rarely picked up a paint brush until Alan, his wife Susie and daughter Ginny (his other daughter Mandy is married and lives with her husband Adrian in Sheffield) moved out of the city of Norwich into the countryside in 1993. They moved to a little village called East Lexham in the heart of Norfolk. The village was very peaceful and pretty. This helped inspire Alan to take up watercolour painting once again.

In 2004 they moved to another small West Norfolk village near Downham Market where they still live today. In 2008 Alan had to retire due to ill health (bad knees) and whilst he still painted regularly he began to spend more and more time gardening. In 2013 his wife Susie suggested that he kept a gardening diary to record his adventures in the garden and capture the changing seasons, animals, birds and the successes and failures of being a gardener he encountered. By the following year Susie suggested that he should write a book from his diary and include illustrations of both the garden and his artwork.

In 2014 Alan's first book was published by Creative Gateway called **"Retiring to the Garden – Year One".** This proved such a success that Alan decided to follow this up with his second book called **"Retiring into a Rainbow"** featuring his watercolour paintings. In 2015 Alan published **"Retiring to Our Garden – Year Two"** published this time by Rainbow Publications UK. He then re-issued his first two books this time in a **"Second Edition"**. Also published by Rainbow Publications UK.

In 2016 Alan published: **"Skiathos a Greek Island Paradise", "Norfolk the County of my Birth", "Art Inspired by a Rainbow", "Ibiza Island of Dreams", "Majorca Island in the Sun", "Flip-flops and Shades on Thassos", "Mardle and a Troshin' in Norfolk", "England the Country of my Birth", "Mousehole the Cornish Jewel", "Sunshine and Shades on Kefalonia", "Shades and Flip-flops on Zakynthos"** and finally **"Trips into my Mind's Eye"** Also published by Rainbow Publications UK..

In 2017, 2018 and 2019 Alan published the following new books entitled: **"Corfu and Mainland Greece", "Crete and the Island of Santorini", "Cyprus the Pyramids and the Holy Land", "Greek Islands in the Sun", "Being Greek - The Culture of the People of Greece", "Greece Land of Gods and Men"** and finally **"Alan's Art Books".** Also published by Rainbow Publications UK…

Books by the same Author

Retiring to the Garden – Year 1

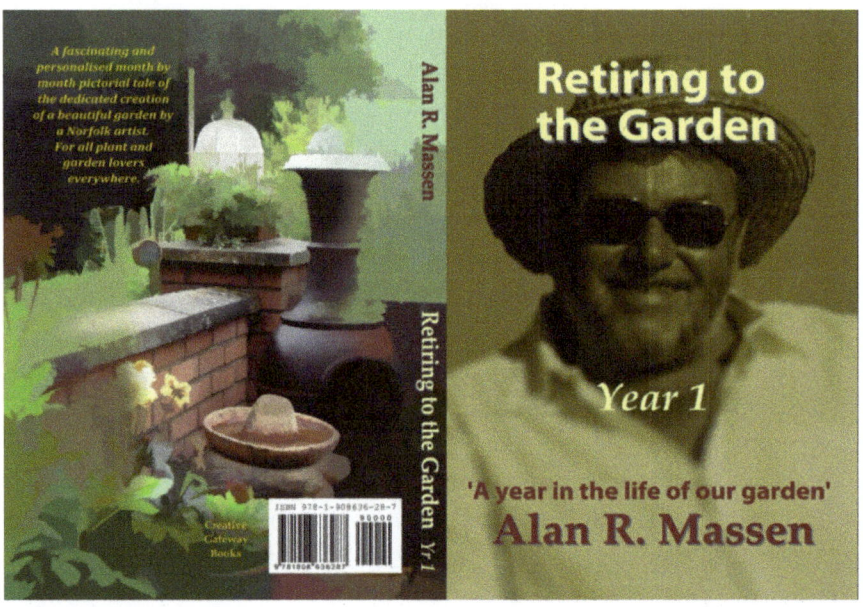

Retiring to Our Garden – Year 1 - 2nd Edition

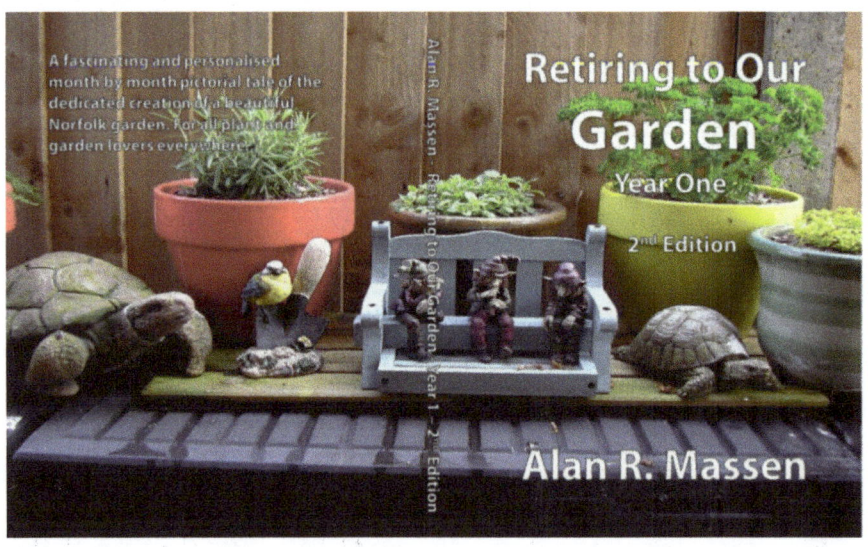

by Norfolk watercolour artist - Alan R. Massen.
Published in Great Britain by Creative Gateway and Rainbow Publications UK

Books by the same Author

Retiring into a Rainbow - 2nd Edition

Retiring to Our Garden – Year Two

by Norfolk watercolour artist - Alan R. Massen.
Published 1st Edition by Creative Gateway and 2nd Edition by Rainbow Publications UK

Books by the same Author

Skiathos a Greek Island Paradise

Norfolk the County of my Birth

by Norfolk watercolour artist - Alan R. Massen.
Published in Great Britain by Rainbow Publications UK

Books by the same Author

Ibiza Island of Dreams

Majorca Island in the Sun

By Norfolk Watercolour Artist - Alan R. Massen
Published in Great Britain by Rainbow Publications UK

Books by the same Author

Art Inspired by a Rainbow

Flip-flops and Shades on Thassos

by Norfolk Watercolour Artist - Alan R. Massen
Published in Great Britain by Rainbow Publications UK

Books by the same Author

Mardle and a Troshin' in Norfolk

Being Greek - The Culture of the People of Greece

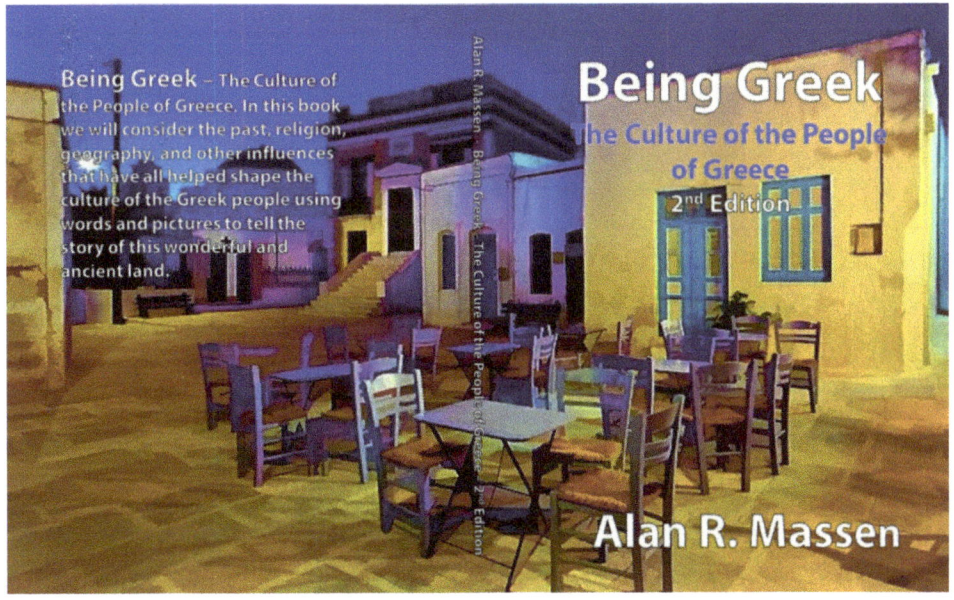

by Norfolk Watercolour Artist - Alan R. Massen
Published in Great Britain by Rainbow Publications UK

Books by the same Author

England the Country of my Birth

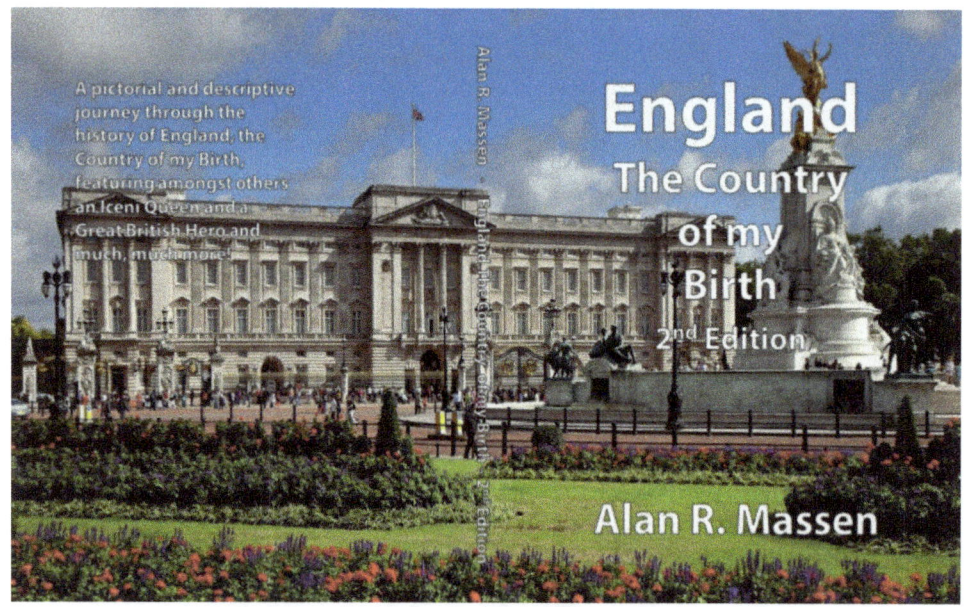

Greek Islands in the Sun

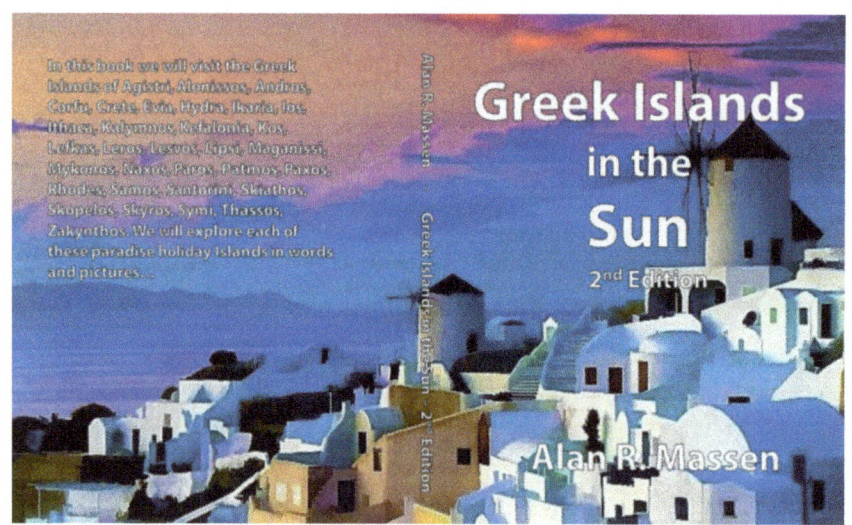

by Norfolk Watercolour Artist - Alan R. Massen
Published in Great Britain by Rainbow Publications UK

Books by the same Author

Mousehole the Cornish Jewel

Crete and the Island of Santorini

by Norfolk Watercolour Artist - Alan R. Massen
Published in Great Britain by Rainbow Publications UK

Books by the same Author

Sunshine and Shades on Kefalonia

Shades and Flip-flops on Zakynthos

by Norfolk Watercolour Artist - Alan R. Massen
Published in Great Britain by Rainbow Publications UK

Books by the same Author

Corfu and Mainland Greece

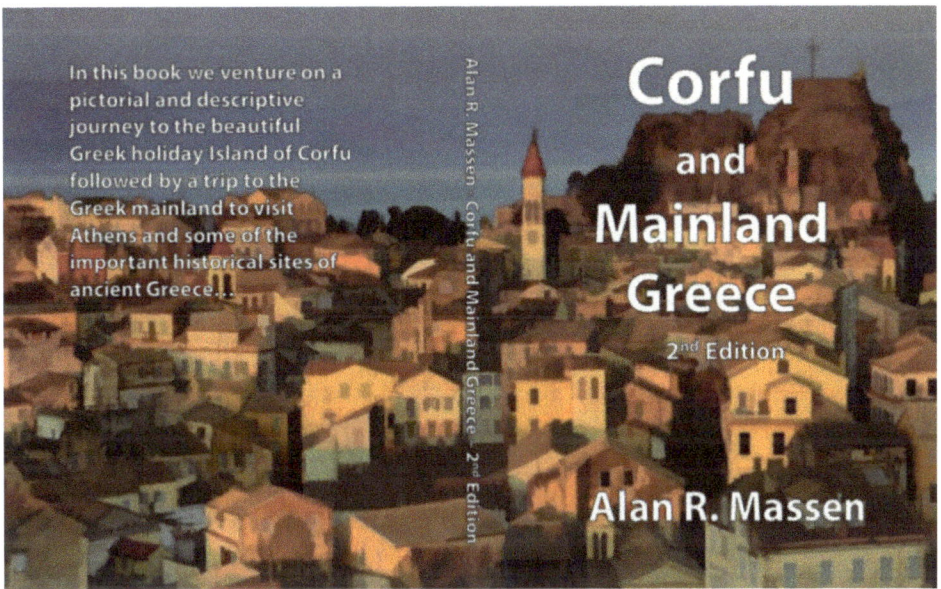

Cyprus the Pyramids and the Holy Land

by Norfolk Watercolour Artist - Alan R. Massen
Published in Great Britain by Rainbow Publications UK

Books by the same Author

Trips into my Minds Eye

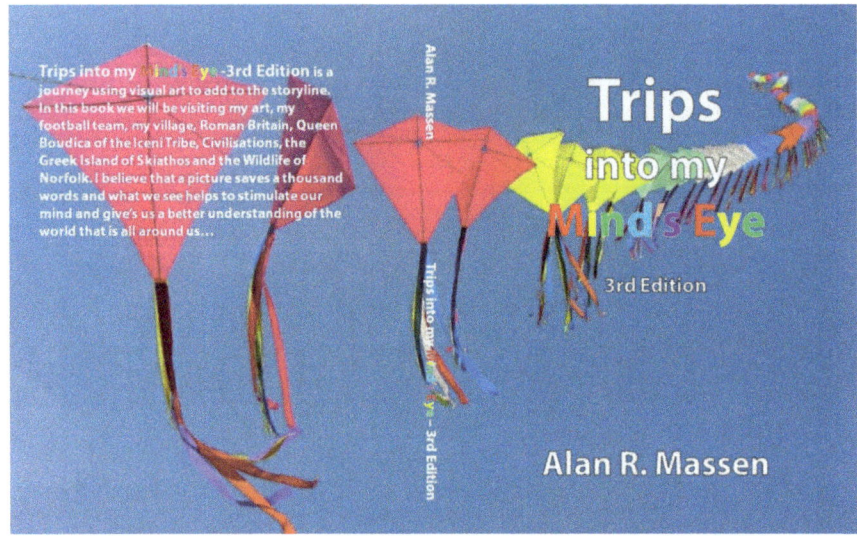

Greece Land of Gods and Men

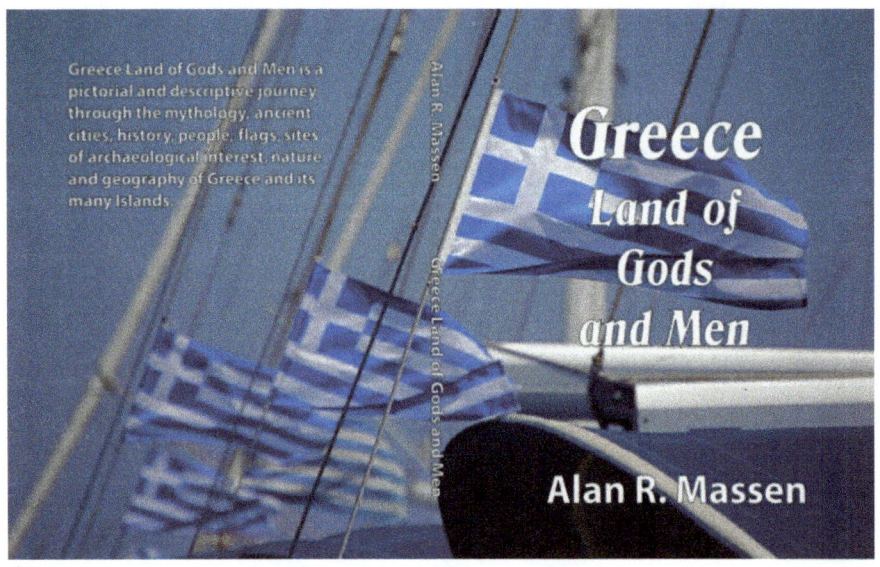

by Norfolk Watercolour Artist - Alan R. Massen
Published in Great Britain by Rainbow Publications UK

Dedication

I would like to dedicate this book to my wife Susie who accompanies me on all of our journeys around the UK and abroad and helps me to enjoy fully every single day of my life.

Corfu…

Latest books by the same Author

Alan's Art Books

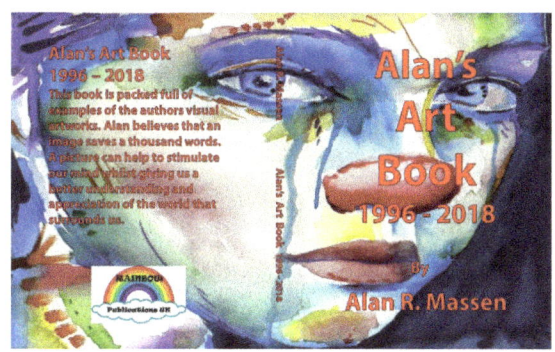 

by Norfolk Watercolour Artist - Alan R. Massen
Published in Great Britain by Rainbow Publications UK

Contents

Introduction	1
The History of Corfu	7
The Geography of Corfu	15
Out and About on Corfu	18
Facts about Corfu	28
Corfu Town	64
A - Z of Corfu Beaches	68
The Best Beaches on Corfu	109
Mainland Greece	164
Being Greek	170
Acknowledgement	202

Copyright © 2019 Alan R. Massen

Introduction

Introduction:

The Island of Corfu is part of Greece which is a country located in south-east Europe located between the Mediterranean and the Aegean Seas. Greece includes many Islands such as Rhodes, Crete, Skiathos, Kefalonia, Ithaca, Thassos, Zakynthos and Corfu. There is a wealth of accommodation in Greece to suit all travellers. There are many great places to visit on mainland Greece and its many paradise Islands. In Greece there is something for everyone with a wealth of historic sites, villages, towns, cities, mountains, sporting venues, walking trails, museums, landmarks, monuments, festivals, carnivals, nature, shopping, great beaches and all set in magnificent surroundings. In this book we will be visiting the great beaches, towns and villages on the lovely Paradise Island of Corfu before travelling to the mainland of Greece itself to visit many of its glorious ancient sites and then onto the City of Athens. In the pages of this book you will see numerous examples of my watercolour paintings and photographic artwork which I have scanned onto my computer. Then using a piece of art software, to give the pictures an impressionist style finish, a bit like the artist Claude Monet, to produce the illustrations used throughout this book. So if you are ready, we will start our journey together…

Introduction:

Greece and the Island of Corfu…

So now we know where the Island of Corfu is and before we venture too far into the pages of this book, I thought, that I ought to introduce myself for those of you that have not been with me on one of my many other journeys to visit other Greek Islands. Hello my name is Alan and I am married to Susie and we live in a small village in North West Norfolk in the UK. Over the last twenty years, we have been fortunate enough to have had numerous summer holidays abroad. Our holiday destination of choice, over the years, has usually been to go to one of the many Greek Islands and/or the mainland of Greece. We have over the years holidayed on the Greek mainland and on many of the Greek Island such as Corfu, Ithaca, Zakynthos, Crete, Santorini, Thassos, Kefalonia and Skiathos to name but a few. We have also visited the major archaeological sites on the mainland of Greece as well as spending several days visiting the important sites in the City of Athens itself. Now that we have been introduced and you know who I am let's return to my introduction to the beautiful paradise Greek Island of Corfu…

Introduction:

Corfu is one of the Ionian Islands off the North-West coast of Greece (39°40 N 19°45 E). Corfu is one of the most Northern Ionian Islands. Many are surprised to learn that the coast directly opposite Corfu is not Greece, but the country of Albania. The narrow channel between Corfu and Albania, is in some places, less than 2 km wide. Generally, the sea on the East and North of Corfu is shallower (light blue) whereas the sea on the Western side of the Island of Corfu is very deep (dark blue)…

Introduction:

Corfu is the second largest of the Greek Ionian Islands and one of the most popular with tourists, Corfu almost resembles the shape of a bent leg (with a little imagination) and lies on the western coast of mainland Greece, within the Ionian Sea. As I have already mentioned the Island of Corfu is very close to the Albanian coastline…

Introduction:

Summary of the holiday Island of Corfu (also known as Kerkyra) is that it is the second-biggest of Greece's Ionian Islands, after the Island of Kefalonia. Corfu is located on the western side of mainland Greece and has an especially green and lush interior, with endless wild flowers, thriving olive groves, vineyards, many tall Cypress trees and endless dreamy, secluded sandy beaches. The Island of Corfu remains one of the most beautiful of all the Greek Islands and is a leading tourist destination in its own right…

Introduction:

The Island of Corfu enjoys a mild Mediterranean climate along with excellent beaches all of which makes it a popular destination for holiday makers. Corfu is very green compared to other Greek Islands. It has hot and dry summers along with winter rain that helps create lush vegetation which is dominated by over 2 million olive trees. These olive trees on Corfu are the main crop cultivated on the Island, although Corfu's tourism now provides the most income for the Islanders. Now that we have completed our introductions let us begin our journey together by learning something about the history of the Island of Corfu…

The History of Corfu

The Island of Corfu has seen a colourful past where Greek, Roman, Venetian and French occupations have left their mark, including two forts. Many Greek myths and legends feature the Island of Corfu including: Hercules, Homer, Odysseus and Jason and his Argonauts. Not surprisingly, Corfu Town is on the UNESCO World Heritage List which has helped to protect and preserve the Towns architecture and monuments…

The History of Corfu:

Corfu history is shorter than that of many other Greek Islands, although it is certainly no less impressive. Over the centuries the Island has played host to all of the major powers, including the Romans, the Venetians and even the British, and has only actually been under Greek rule for a relatively short amount of time. The Island of Corfu has quite a different look and feel to much of the rest of Greece, and has a notable lack of archaeological sites…

The History of Corfu:

The history of the Island of Corfu (named Kerkyra in Greek) goes back to the 8th century BC, when it was called Corcyra. Due to its positioning near the mouth of the Adriatic Sea, Corfu Town became a naval base and trade centre under the Corinthians. It eventually split from Corinth (on mainland Greece). The Island then entered into a century long conflict, before being conquered by Macedonia and placed under its wing. Relics from these early years can be found at the Corfu Archaeological Museum in Corfu Town...

The History of Corfu:

The Romans

The Romans claimed the Island of Corfu in the year 229 BC. They then set about the building of their bathhouses, villas and roads, and were on the Island for some 500 years (right up until 337 AD). The Romans used the Island's port to conduct campaigns into the Eastern Mediterranean. The Byzantine Empire took over when the Roman Empire was in its decline and that tenure lasted right into the 13th century…

The History of Corfu:

The Byzantines

The Byzantines fortified Corfu town from pirate attacks, with many of these towers remaining on the Island today. The Old Fortress in Corfu Town was started in the 8th century and was enhanced by both the Venetians and the British during their respective stays on the Island. The fort today is Corfu Town's main ancient tourist attraction along with the nearby New Fortress, or 'Neo Frourio'…

The History of Corfu:

Alexander the Great

The Norman and Venetians

The Normans ruled the Island of Corfu prior to its takeover by the Venetians. A period of unrest pitted the French King of Sicily against the Venetians, although Venice controlled Corfu fully right up until the late 18th century. At this time, numerous olive trees were planted in the fertile soil and these still dot the Island today. The Venetians also erected many fine, classical-style buildings on the Island. One of these is the Church of Agios Spyridon in the heart of the historic Corfu Town, which dates from the late 1580's and it frequently functions as a popular meeting place for tourists. The Old Town has a very Venetian air in general and it is a pleasant spot to stroll around, with winding pedestrianised alleys and a wide seafront esplanade…

The History of Corfu:

Ottoman Turks and British Rule

The Ottomans then ruled the Island until the French leader Napoleon came here in 1797. At that time much of Greece was under the Turks. The French were then driven off the Island by the Russians, then the Russians by the Turks and finally the Turks by the British in 1800, with the latter occupying the Island of Corfu fully in 1815 and developing roads and improvements to the education of the population on the Island. The Island then witnessed the construction of the very English-style Palace of St. Michael and St. Georges that commenced in 1819, followed by the Royal Gardens. The Ionian Islands, including the Island of Corfu, joined Greece in 1864, almost 30 years after gaining independence from Turkey and British rule…

The History of Corfu:

Ancient Greek Sailing Boat

The Island of Corfu Today

Once under the rule of the Greek nation, many fine buildings were erected on the Island of Corfu, including the Achillion Palace. The history of the Island of Corfu includes being involved in both World Wars, with its capital town sustaining heavy bomb damage in WWII, including the loss of its library, theatre, and the Ionian Academy. The town was subsequently rebuilt after the war and the Island was quick to get back on its feet by enticing tourists and succeeding in becoming a hot holiday destination. The resorts nearest Corfu Town are amongst the Island's busiest beaches, being well-placed as they are for visits to the historic capital Town of the Island. Having completed our brief history of the Island we now move on and in the next chapter we will look at the geography of the Island…

The Geography of Corfu

On the Island of Corfu the northern region is fairly wide and mountainous, with a number of pleasant pebbly beaches strung along its coastline, while the southern region of the Island generally features the most popular and varied sandy beaches and resorts on the Island…

The Geography of Corfu:

Offering something very different to the sandy and/or pebble beaches of the Island of Corfu are the Island's historic landmarks. In Corfu Town itself, both the Old Fortress (Palaio Frourio) and the New Fortress (Neo Frourio) are of great interest and provide some extraordinary views, thanks in no small part to their elevated settings. The Royal Gardens at the Palaia Anaktora are especially inviting, as are the gardens next to the Achillion Palace, in the region of Gastouri. Another very important landmark on Corfu is the Palace of St. Michael and St. Georges, which is home to the Municipal Art Gallery, which houses art works and information about the Roman and Byzantine periods and much, much more…

The Geography of Corfu:

A friendly dog we met in Assos on the Island of Kefalonia

For many, the unique experiences offered on the Island of Corfu are reason enough to stay here for their entire holiday. Others find the proximity of several other famous Greek Islands just too tempting, with ferries linking Corfu to other Ionian destinations such as the Islands of Kefalonia, Erikoussa, Othoni and also Zakynthos (Zante). The Island of Kefalonia is especially nearby to Corfu and makes for the perfect day trip, offering visitors great beaches, vineyards, mountain trails and plenty of history, within both its capital Town of Argostoli and its main Port of Sami. Now that we have explored some of the geography and places of interest on this lovely Island we will, in the next chapter go out and about on the Island of Corfu…

Out and About on Corfu

Some useful information about the Island of Corfu

Corfu Population: 110,000 approximately - Capital: Corfu Town (Kerkyra)
Corfu Island Size: 597 km² (63 km Long and 28 km Wide)
Corfu Highest Mountain: Mount Pantokratoras (906 m)
Coastline of Corfu: 217 km
Number of Beaches on Corfu: 92 (Sandy and Shingle)
Language Spoken on Corfu: Greek (English is also very commonly spoken)…

Out and About:

You should always find time for a coffee in Greece

Corfu Town is the Island's rather sophisticated and charming capital and locally goes by the name of 'Kastropolis', due to its location, with two large fortresses standing either side of the town. The town's 'Liston' promenade is a major visitor attraction here, as is the adjacent Spainada (Esplanade), the main plaza. In the summer months visitors can get Island and Town maps from a tourist kiosk which is open on the Plateia San Rocco. The Island of Corfu is home to a population of just over 110,000 people, around 30,000 Islanders live within Corfu Town, the capital. Corfu Town is situated on the eastern coast of the Island's central section, and is divided into two main regions, north and south Town…

Out and About:

The Island of Corfu is home to some of the most glorious beaches that the Ionian Islands have to offer, a large number of tourists, who visit and stay on Corfu, rarely leave the beaches, spending their time relaxing in the sun and swimming in the warm clear sea. The Island's main activities tend to related to its coastline and if you have not arrived with your own private yacht, you may be interested in chartering a yacht for the day. Many of the lively beaches are very close to Corfu Town itself or around this part of the eastern coast, while to the south, Benites village and beach is a thriving and very popular resort. Western Corfu features some if the Island's prettiest beaches and countryside, particularly around the seaside village of Paleokastritsa. The choice of beaches is almost endless, with those next to the busiest resorts tending to be the most developed, with good facilities and fine food…

Out and About:

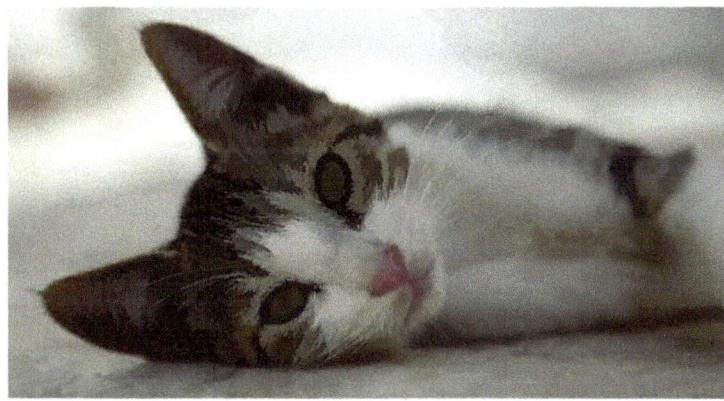

Ioannis Kapodistrias International Airport

Flying to the Island of Corfu, for most Europeans, is an easy flight lasting less than 3 hours. Corfu's International airport (Kapodistrias) is located on the edge of Corfu (Kerkyra) town. It is a very modern and compact airport. During the summer months (May to October) there are regular charter flights from most European countries to Corfu. Domestic flights (from Athens) operate all the year round. Corfu Airport features a single terminal, which efficiently handles all of its passengers and air traffic, and can become especially busy during the summer months of July and August, when large numbers of holidaymakers arrive on the Island…

Out and About:

Ioannis Kapodistrias International Airport

The Airport is housed in a small but modern building, Corfu Ioannis Kapodistrias International Airport (CFU) is busy for its size, operating around three flights a day to Athens and several additional international flights to a number of other international airports including Austria, Germany and the UK. The airport can be found just a short distance from Corfu Town itself, which lies some 3 km / 2 miles to the north. Operating a single terminal, the airport becomes extremely busy when holiday makers flock to the Island in large numbers. Domestic flights come from Greek airports, although the majority of the summer air traffic comprises of charter flights from many package holiday providers and foreign airlines…

Out and About:

Ioannis Kapodistrias International Airport

The airport is sited close to Kerkyra, Pontikonisi, Potamos and the beautiful Vlaheraina Monastery. When arriving and departing, passengers are treated to spectacular views across Pontikonisi, the Kanoni hills and the coastline. A large number of holiday makers who fly into Corfu's Ioannis Kapodistrias Airport choose to hire a car when they arrive, and this form of transport is especially popular with young families. Rental cars allow you to travel all over Corfu with relative ease, and since this is a very large Island, the road network between the main resorts is excellent. Bus transport is also very popular with tourists and buses travel around Corfu Town itself, and further afield, to most areas and resorts on the Island. Ferry and hydrofoil services are also available, should you wish to travel around the coastline or visit another Island for the day, or even longer during your holiday stay…

Out and About:

Driving to Corfu

Some people even drive from their home all the way to the Island of Corfu, the regular ferries from Italy and the Greek mainland to Corfu can make the trip easier to plan. The roads of Corfu are generally in good condition, even if unavoidably steep and twisting in some locations due to its mountainous terrain. Car and motorcycle hire companies are plentiful within Corfu Town and also in the other Island resorts. These mode of transport offers the visitor by far the greatest freedom, allowing them to travel between the many beaches and resorts. As you travel around the Island of Corfu by car or motorcycle, the Island's two main motorways (the GR-24 to Paleokastritsa and the GR-25 to Lefkimi) are a good point of reference and may well allow you to reach your destination a little quicker than you would have expected…

Out and About:

Buses and Coaches

Long-distance bus transport on the Island of Corfu is operated by 'KTEL'. Often referred to locally as the ' green buses', visitors will find that the KTEL buses are one of the easiest and cheapest ways to travel around the Island, with buses departing from Corfu Town's bus station and travelling all over the Island, to destinations and resorts such as:

Agios Gordios (45 minutes) - Agios Stefanos (one hour and 30 minutes)
Aharavi (one hour and 15 minutes) - Arillas (one hour and 15 minutes)
Barbati (45 minutes) - Ermones (30 minutes) - Glyfada (30 minutes)
Kassiopi (45 minutes) - Kavos (one hour and 30 minutes)
Messonghi (45 minutes) - Paleokastritsa (45 minutes) - Pyrgi (30 minutes)
Sidhari (one hour and 15 minutes) - Spartera (45 minutes)

The local Islands short distance buses are known on Corfu as ' blue buses'. Tickets for these buses can be purchased from the ticket booth on the Plateia San Rocco, although some tickets may be purchased on the buses themselves, including those headed for the villages of Ahillion, Benitses and Kouramades…

Out and About:

Boats and Ferries

Corfu's port is at the edge of Corfu (Kerkyra) Town. Ferries from the Greek mainland (Igumenitsa and Patra) offer a regular ferry service as well as ferries from as far away as Italy (Venice, Ancona and Brindisi) call in at the port. The Island of Corfu port is also a popular stop for visiting cruise ships. During the summer season, ferry and hydrofoil transportation seems to be coming and going in and out of the port all of the time. The most popular routes from Corfu's port include Igoumenitsa, Lefkimmi, Paxos (Paxi), Patra and the Albanian city of Saranda, with daily sailings being regularly available. High-speed ferries named 'Flying Dolphins' are particularly fast and therefore are very popular. As we have seen ferries even travel to the Island of Corfu from as far afield as Bari and Venice in Italy making the port very busy…

Out and About:

Olive tree…

The black nets for under the olive trees:

They are used to collect ripe olives. The locals that do not earn a living from tourism, often turn to Olive production. There are an estimated 3 million Olive trees on Corfu. It is no wonder that the Island is so green!

The country opposite Corfu:

The land opposite Corfu is the country of Albania! Few of Corfu's first-time visitors, realise how close the previous communist state of Albania is. In places it is less than 2 miles across the water. Today it is quite safe though! Many years ago, there were reports of 'Albanian Pirates' swimming across to steal boats from local Corfiots. It is now unheard of. If you are really intrigued, it is possible to go on a local ferry (from Corfu town) and visit Albania for the day.

There is another Corfu:

Did you know there is a small town in the American state of New York called Corfu? It was named after the Ionian Island of Corfu in 1839 by the founder of the local post office. Now that we have been out and about it is now time, in the next chapter, to find out some more facts about the lovely Paradise Island of Corfu…

Facts about Corfu

The Island of Corfu is a tourist hotspot

The seemingly endless sunny weather of the Greek climate has resulted in the Island of Corfu becoming nothing short of a tourist hotspot and is one of the most popular of the Greek Islands in the Ionian Sea. The climate of the Island of Corfu is quite different to that of mainland Greece, with its infrequent periods of heavy rain resulting in particularly lush vegetation. During the summer months, Corfu and the many other Ionian Islands can enjoy an extremely hot summer climate, with many holiday makers choosing to sunbathe on the beaches, and cool down in the crystal clear seawater. July and August regularly see temperatures of more than 31°C / 88°F, on the Island it is not uncommon to see highs topping 40°C / 104°F and the Island remaining almost completely without rainfall throughout this period. Corfu's tourist season is from early May until the end of October. The hottest (and driest) months being July and August where the temperature will often reach 35° centigrade. Some tourists do visit the Island of Corfu in the winter months and although mild, it can often be very wet …

Facts about Corfu:

The Weather of Corfu

The Island of Corfu does not experience the cooling breeze of the mainland Greece's 'meltemi' winds. Corfu instead gets the northern Ionian Sea 'maistro' breezes that offer very pleasant, cooling breezes in the height of the summer climate, particularly during June and July. The Island of Corfu with its perfect beaches, weather and warm evenings is a firm favourite with holiday makers. The summer climate is a little too hot for some people and many prefer to holiday on Corfu during May, which marks the very beginning of the tourist season. Visiting the Islands in May has the distinct advantage that the beaches are less crowded, the tavernas are much quieter and the Island is awash with colourful flowers everywhere. The mild October weather in Corfu and even the Ionian winters are mild, although this is generally considered to be the wet season between November and March…

Facts about Corfu:

Where to stay on Corfu

The Island of Corfu has a wide range of holiday accommodation available to suit most pockets. Corfu is popular with all kinds of visitors, particularly couples and families. Many hotels are right next to some of Corfu's most beautiful sandy beaches and have wonderful sea views. On Corfu, even during the busy summer season, there are plenty of hotels that offer very competitive rates. Many of the Island's best hotels are concentrated around Corfu Town itself, However, many visitors prefer to look for accommodation in the towns more characterful Old Town area…

Facts about Corfu:

Where to stay on Corfu

North of Corfu Town, the accommodation can only be described as variable, so do try to choose your hotel very carefully.

Kassiopi is an especially popular and very lively tourist resort and its pebbly beachfront is always thronging with tourists. A real favourite for many people visiting the Island is the White House in Kalami, which features just eight guest rooms and is actually the former residence of the famous novelist Lawrence Durrell. Head to the south of Corfu Town and hotels are based around the resorts of Benitses, and the town of Lefkimmi. The west coast is home to some of Corfu's most attractive villages and countryside, with hotels close to the beaches of Agios Georgios, Glyfada, Myrtiotissa and Pelekas, and around the beautiful beach resort town of Paleokastritsa, where accommodation often comes complete with a glorious view of the cliffs, bays, the clear blue sea and green olive groves…

Facts about Corfu:

Places to visit on Corfu

If lying on Corfu's sun drenched beaches, or lazing by the hotel pool, is not your scene, do not worry. The Island of Corfu has much more to offer. Corfu Island boasts Mount Pantokrator, which is over 1000 meters high, offering breath-taking views across to the nearby Island of Paxos. There is also the old town of Kerkyra which is a must visit for all Island visitors. Many of the most popular tourist attractions on the Island of Corfu are to be found around the main beach resorts and coastline. The Old Town is full of character and some of Corfu Town's oldest attractions, whilst those holidaying with young families will no doubt enjoying spending time splashing around at Aqua-land of building sandcastles on one of the beautiful Island beaches…

Facts about Corfu:

Places to visit on Corfu

On the Island of Corfu much of the action is to be found within the resorts of Benitses, the village of Roda, and the beautiful resort of Paleokastritsa, where the Moni Theotokou monastery resides. The golfers amongst you may be interested in playing a round at the Corfu Golf Club, which lies on the western coast, to the south of the Paleokastritsa, close to Ermones Beach…

Facts about Corfu:

Moni Theotokou Monastery

Places to visit on Corfu

As already mentioned the monastery known as the Moni Theotokou can be found on Corfu's west coast, within the resort of Paleokastritsa. Established as far back as the 13th century, the monastery building here today was actually built during the 18th century and contains a detailed picture showing the Last Judgement. The outside walls of the Moni Theotokou monastery are whitewashed and draped in bougainvillea, which is truly a magnificent sight to behold when it is in full flower. In Paleokastritsa itself there are plenty of sandy beaches to enjoy…

Facts about Corfu:

Places to visit on Corfu

The Old Town area of Corfu Town is particularly enchanting and contains a number of appealing historical attractions that have a distinctive Venetian flavour. Much of the Old Town comprises of a maze-like array of cobblestone alleyways and these winding streets are known locally as the 'kantounia'. In Town the Venetian Citadel is a particular highlight for many visitors, as is the seafront esplanade with its sea views across the Bay of Garitsa. Close to the historic Venetian Citadel in Corfu Town is a large central square, which is separated into two main areas by an intersecting street. The Upper Square is referred to locally as the 'Ano Platei' and the enormous Lower Square which is known by the name of the 'Kato Plateia'. It is reputed to be amongst the largest plazas in the whole of south-east Europe. A number of noteworthy attractions surround the Kato Plateia, such as various green open spaces, seasonal flowers, a Romani-influenced rotunda, and a rather gorgeous music pavilion, where regularly performances by the town's Philharmonic Orchestra (Philharmoniki) are staged which are well worth looking out for…

Facts about Corfu:

Aqua-Land

One of the very best of all the family orientated tourist attractions on Corfu is the Aqua-land and is highly recommended as it offers the ultimate way to cool down on a hot summer's day. Aqua-land truly does offer something for everyone, with a beach area with sun loungers for those who simply want to lay back and relax, along with enormous water slides, 'free fall' slides, a winding lazy river, a giant Jacuzzi, and a shallow pool for younger children to enjoy, which comes complete with its own mini octopus and frog. There is even an adventure playground, bouncy castle and arcade with the latest video games, along with a site restaurant, a bar, and ice cream shops selling Greek-style 'gelateria'. It is quite likely that you will spend an entire day in Aqua-land, particularly if you come to the Island with young children…

Facts about Corfu:

The Resort of Benitses

Benitses is one of the resorts that I stayed in when I visited Corfu on one of our summer holidays to the Island. It is a small town sited roughly 12 km / 7 miles to the south of Corfu Town. The narrow streets are full of shops, bars and tavernas that all provide a certain charm to Benitses. Benitses is home to a couple of narrow, sandy beaches along the seafront, either side of its centrally located harbour. Other attractions include a pleasant walking trail through the nearby valley to the 'water springs', while some may like to visit the Benitses Shell Museum, where there are fossils, sharks' teeth and a collection of weird creatures found in the surrounding seawater…

Facts about Corfu:

The Resort of Roda

The highly characterful village of Roda resides on the northerly coastline of Corfu and originally started life as nothing more than a small fishing village. These days, Roda has been somewhat swallowed up by the Island's flourishing tourist industry and its main attractions, tavernas and souvenir shops tend to be based along the resorts waterfront. The beach is nice and many holiday makers enjoy hiring small motorboats to explore the Islands coastline at their leisure. Also the remaining fishing harbour, which is located on the eastern side of the beach is worth wandering around. The resort of Roda is famous for its busy nightlife…

Facts about Corfu:

The Corfu Golf Club

The Corfu Golf Club offers something completely different, away from the beach resorts, bars and shops. Also close to the hilltop village of Pelekas, the Golf Club boasts an especially impressive course, which is reputed to be amongst Europe's most beautiful. The landscape around the golf course consists of woodland, lakes, meandering streams and excellent views, while for many, a great meal in the spacious clubhouse after a round of golf is not to be missed…

Facts about Corfu:

The Old Fortress Corfu Town

Landmarks and Monuments on Corfu

Contrasting greatly with the tourist scene around the beaches of Corfu are the Island's historic landmarks and monuments. One of the most famous of all the landmarks on the Island of Corfu is the Old Fortress which is known locally in Greek as the Palaio Frourio and is standing on an adjacent Island and is surrounded by imposing fortifications. Palaio Frourio (Old Fortress / Citadel): The interior of the Palaio Frourio remains in a very good state of repair and is often used to host a number of Corfu's leading events and concerts, with the background being provided by none other than the Aegean Sea itself. The centre of the fortress features a tall obelisk structure, with its very own observation area at the very top. The Neo Frourio (New Fortress / Citadel) is often referred to by tourists as either the New Fortress or the New Citadel, the Neo Frourio stands alongside the coastline, on the north-eastern side of Corfu Town. With enormous walls surrounding the entire landmark, the Neo Frourio dominates the waterfront and is open to members of the general public, who can learn more about the history of the fortress by taking a guided tour around the medieval passageways and corridors. A treat not to be missed…

Facts about Corfu:

Sunset in Corfu Town

Landmarks and Monuments on Corfu

The Palaia Anaktora (Old Palaces) and the Royal Gardens (Garden of the People) is sited on the northern side of the Kato Plateia, the Palaia Anaktora comprises of an extensive complex of historical, Romanesque buildings and palaces, surrounded by Venetian fortifications and castle-like turrets. Used in the past to house everyone from the British Governors to the King of Greece. The Palaia Anaktora contains a series of large halls and corridors, where various art works are displayed. The gardens of the palaces are named the Royal Gardens and are especially impressive, being filled with exotic planting schemes and seasonal colour. The gardens gives the visitor some superb views of the bay and of the surrounding area …

Facts about Corfu:

Cheeky Statue ! In the grounds of the Achillion-Palace

Landmarks and Monuments on Corfu

The Achilleion / Achillion Palace is located off the coastal road to the south of Corfu Town, the Achillion Palace is another important Corfu monument and is conveniently close to the villages of Gastouri and Benitses. Also worth looking out for are the landmarks of the Palaia Anaktora, the Church of Agios Spyridon, Kaiser's Bridge, and the Palace of St. Michael and St. Georges, which were completed in 1824. During the latter part of the 19th century, this beautiful landmark building the Achilleion / Achillion Palace served as the summertime palace for the Austrian Empress Elizabeth (Sissy). Take a walk around the formally landscaped garden surrounding the Achillion Palace, and look out for the various statues of mythological characters, including the legendary Greek hero of the Trojan war, Achilles, the palace's namesake. Also be sure to climb up the stairs in the garden to enjoy the views from the marble terrace. After Empress Elizabeth's tragic assassination in 1898, the palace remained deserted for almost a decade, before being purchased by the German Kaiser Wilhelm II. Kaiser Wilhelm II was extremely fond of the Island and often holidayed on Corfu. Following his acquisition of the Achillion Palace, Wilhelm commissioned the redesigning of the palace's botanical gardens and the surrounding area. To enable him to be able to reach the beach with ease, without the need to cross the road itself, Kaiser Wilhelm ordered that a stone bridge be built, to connect the Achillion gardens with the nearby beachfront. This bridge remains as a monument to the Kaiser's wealth and self-importance, although the central section was actually removed by the Germans during WWII, to allow their vehicles greater access to the road itself…

Facts about Corfu:

Landmarks and Monuments on Corfu

There are almost 40 different churches spread around the Island of Corfu, the Church of Agios Spyridon is without question the Island's most important and was built more than 400 years ago. Dedicated to the Island's patron saint 'Agios Spyridon', the church's bell tower is easily visible from all around the busy Kantounia area of the town and beyond, and therefore serves as a very useful point of reference and also a convenient meeting place. The Palace of St. Michael and St. Georges appears more like a stately home on an English estate, than a Greek palace on the resort Island of Corfu. The Palace of St. Michael and St. Georges boasts impressive Neo-classical architecture and a Maltese marble facade, and resides on the northerly side of the Spianada, within Corfu Town itself. The palace served as the official residence of the British Lord High Commissioners. In subsequent years, the Palace of St. Michael and St. Georges become a summer retreat for the Greek monarchy and today houses both the Museum of Asian Art and the Municipal Art Gallery…

Facts about Corfu:

Gorgon Medusa Sculpture

The Museums and Art Galleries of Corfu

When visiting the Island of Corfu and for a pleasant change from sunbathing on the beach you could indulge in a day of culture by visiting any of the Island's numerous museums. The majority of the main museums and galleries are to be found within Corfu Town itself, and they cover topics such as Asian art, archaeology, religion and history, amongst others. The Island's acclaimed Archaeological Museum is home to an interesting and extensive collection of Island artefacts, that shows Corfu's very rich archaeological heritage. A real highlight at the museum is the enormous Gorgon Medusa sculpture, which is of great historical significance, being amongst the finest remaining archaic sculpture in the whole of Greece today…

Facts about Corfu:

Greek Religion Wheel

The Museums and Art Galleries of Corfu

The Archaeological Museum has many good exhibits, such as the Gorgon Medusa sculpture which was unearthed in the Temple of Artemis at Corcyra, which is known to date back as far as the 6th century BC. Those visiting the town's Archaeological Museum should also look out for the important relics from the Islands Bronze Age, and the rather impressive collection of coins, which date as far back as the 6th century BC and much, much more…

Facts about Corfu:

The Museums and Art Galleries of Corfu

The Museum of Asian Art is well worth a visit. The Corfu Museum of Asian Art is home to in excess of 10,000 different exhibits, many of which have been donated from private collections. Located within the Palace of Saints Michael and George, the various items on display are very diverse and are spread across 15 rooms. They include porcelain from China and Japan, along with bronzes, screens, paintings and fine sculptures…

Facts about Corfu:

The Dionysos Ariadni Amphora

The Museums and Art Galleries of Corfu

The Byzantine Museum of Corfu (Antivouniotissa Museum) is housed within the 15th-century Church of Our Lady of Antivouniotissa, the Byzantine Museum of Corfu contains a wealth of artefacts and religious art works, dating from between the 13th century and the 17th century. An extension of the collection is also to be found within the sacristy, although the basilica of the church itself is particularly stunning, featuring a dramatic timbered roof…

Facts about Corfu:

The Museums and Art Galleries of Corfu

The Museum of Palaeopolis is on the southerly side of Corfu Town, on the Kanoni Peninsula, within the restored residence of the Mon Repos Estate. The highlights of the museum include various archaeological relics, a ' Period Room', and extensive landscaped gardens, which are home to no less than two Doric temples. The gardens are perfect for having a picnic in, if you bring food with you as there are no refreshments or shop available onsite…

Facts about Corfu:

The Museums and Art Galleries of Corfu

The Solomos Museum (Museum of Dionusios Solomos) is located within a very charming Corfu Town house. The Solomos Museum celebrates the life and works of the famous Greek poet, Dionysius Solomos who lived on the Island for over 30 years, during the 19th century. The poet Dionusios Solomos is known for many of his works, but in particular, is famed for penning the national poem of Greece. Many of his personal belongings are on display here in his former residence, including some original manuscripts, poems, letters, portraits, rare books and the actual desk he used to pen his works…

Facts about Corfu:

The Museums and Art Galleries of Corfu

The Municipal Art Gallery is another good Island museum situated within the Palace of Saints Michael and George, the Municipal Art Gallery of Corfu contains a large and impressive collection of art works, created by Corfiot painters and also artists from the 15th-century Byzantine period. These include works by the father and son Prossalendis, and the Cretan Damaskinas. Other museums of interest on the Island of Corfu are the: Benitses Shell Museum, Historical and Folkloric Museum, Kapodistrias Museum, Numismatic Museum and the Serbian Museum…

Facts about Corfu:

Assos on Kefalonia…

Corfu Island Hopping

The glorious beaches of Corfu and their related attractions are usually more than enough to keep holiday makers fully entertained however, due to its convenient location, Corfu is well-placed for Island hopping. The attractions of neighbouring Ionian Islands, such of Erikoussa, Kefalonia, Othoni and Zakynthos (Zante), are really too close to be ignored. From the port in Corfu Town you can visit Sami, on the Island of Kefalonia. It is one of the Island's busiest ports, although it has become most famous recently for being used as a film location in the film Captain Corelli's Mandolin. From the port at Sami you can take another boat to reach the small and perfectly formed Island of Pontikonisi, which is just a few kilometres away and can be reached in literally just a matter of a few minutes. Even the endless attractions of Albania and Italy are within easy reach of the Island of Corfu by ferry…

Facts about Corfu:

Assos on the Island of Kefalonia

Corfu Island Hopping

As we have already seen you can Island hop from Corfu to the Island of Kefalonia which is the biggest of all the Ionian Islands by ferry but you can also fly there. Kefalonia is relatively close to Corfu and perfect for a day trip or brief excursion, with these two Islands being connected by inexpensive daily flights between the two Island airports. Kefalonia hides many secrets and attractions beneath its more prominent, touristy facade of spectacular beaches and resorts. Try to make time to explore one or two of Kefalonia's innumerable vineyards, or enjoy a trek along one of the scenic mountain trails. Argostoli is the capital of Kefalonia, although many other beautiful seaside villages may also be of interest, such as the ones we visited at Assos, Fiskardo and Sami…

Facts about Corfu:

Corfu Island Hopping

The Island of Erikoussa (Ereikoussa) is the most northerly of the Ionian Islands. Erikoussa is so close to Corfu that it is actually considered to be a prefecture of the Island. Also known as Ereikoussa, the Island of Erikoussa has just one town and a limited number of attractions, although the quite beaches of Bragkini and Porto are well worth visiting. The Island of Othoni: is situated directly to the north-west of Corfu and is the westernmost of the Ionian Islands. Othoni is part of the overall Corfu Prefecture and has a population of less than 700 Islanders. There are a number of good beach attractions dotted around Othoni, such as the rather famous caves next to the sands of Aspros Ammos, where legend purports that Calypso once held Ulysses as his captive…

Facts about Corfu:

Corfu Island Hopping

The Island of Pontikonisi (Mouse Island) apart from its green landscape and abundant woodland, the monastery of Pantokrator is the main attraction on Pontikonisi (Mouse Island). It features an eye-catching staircase made of white stones. When it is viewed from a distance, this white staircase almost resembles the tail of a mouse, earning the Island its rather colourful name of 'Mouse Island'. Also within easy reach is the Island of Zakynthos (Zante) is the third-largest of the Ionian Islands. Zakynthos boasts a truly thriving tourist industry, due in no small part to its countless sandy beaches and beautiful, crystal clear seawater. The Island of Zakynthos is also well known in this part of Greece for its exceptional scuba diving opportunities, with many of the best sites being cave dives. Scuba divers exploring the coastline of Zakynthos can expect to encounter everything from octopus and monk seals, to colourful fish and even loggerhead turtles. The Island is also famous for being the location of one of the most photographed locations in the world "Shipwreck Beach" which Susie and I have visited several times in the past…

Facts about Corfu:

The Events and Festivals on Corfu

There are many significant festivals during Corfu's calendar year of events, a large proportion of which are traditional and religious. Some of the other Island's festivals are targeted more at the summer tourists and are very popular. These include open-air concerts and displays of traditional dance. Seasonal festivals are always popular and many take full advantage of the Island's beautiful coastal scenery, being held around the main beach resorts, such as Corfu Town itself (Kerkyra), Agios Georgios and Pelekas. One festival in particular, the mountain village of Agios Mattheos has become known for its outstanding night-long celebrations on August 6th, which should simply not be missed under any circumstances, while the February carnival season is also outstanding on the Island…

Facts about Corfu:

The Events and Festivals on Corfu

The Greek Orthodox celebrations at Easter are always cause for much excitement on Corfu, with marching bands and bright-red decorations used during the time of the 'Early Resurrection'. Each of the Island's village usually holds one or more 'Paniyiri' festivals during the year, where the whole community comes together to celebrate together. Greek traditional paniyiris are held at the villages and towns of Gimari, Lafki, Pantokratoros and Strinilas, and these events tend to be very family orientated. During the summer season, the philharmonic band playing in Corfu Town becomes a particular attraction for many visitors and Corfiotes (locals), with regular weekend concerts being performed at the Spianada Green gazebo. Also popular and held during the month of July is the Island's very popular cricket season, a historical event where cricket matches are held on the Esplanade in Corfu Town. These have taken place for almost the last 200 years…

Facts about Corfu:

The Events and Festivals on Corfu

If you are in Loustri, which is near to Agni Bay, on September 1st and feeling a little hungry then the Pie Festival is sure to be the one for you, with local tavernas baking a huge number of pies (pitas). Other noteworthy events of Corfu include:

Cheese-Eating Sunday - mid-February, in central Corfu Town
All Saints Day - June 3rd, around Agii Douli
Saint Kyriaki Day - July 7th, in Peroulades
Festival of Folklore Dance - mid-July, in Benitses
Festival of Saint Paraskevi - July 26th, in Velonades
Corfu Sardine Festival - mid-August, in Benitses
Varkarola Music Festival - mid-August, at Paleokastritsa
Return of the Virgin from Assumption - August 22nd and 23rd, at Agraphi
Revolution Processions - late October, throughout the Ionian Islands
Corfu St. Spyridon Celebrations - early November…

Facts about Corfu:

Eating Out on the Island of Corfu

The traditional Greek cuisine served at many restaurants and tavernas all over the Island of Corfu has been greatly shaped by history and by many different cultures. It has, for example, been very noticeably influenced by Italian cuisine. There is a great selection of tasty dishes available at restaurant and tavernas on the Island of Corfu which are generally packed with strong flavours, such as garlic and herbs…

Facts about Corfu:

Eating Out on Corfu

When it comes to Greek food they use a lot of olive oil and visitors should really try to experience how a real Greek salad looks and tastes, coming complete with olives, chopped tomatoes, red onion, cucumber and of course a good swig of olive oil, with Feta cheese on the top for good measure. As well as the traditional Greek menu most Corfu restaurants cater very well for visitors who often require a different kind of cuisine. Dining venues around the Island serve everything from pizzas and burgers, to pasta and simple filled rolls. There are a number of popular Greek specialty dishes available on most menus of Greek restaurants and tavernas around the Island of Corfu. It is well worth looking out for the following delights when dining out:

Bourdeto - spicy fish casserole, with paprika
Mezedhes - appetizers or simple snacks from bakeries
Pastitsada - meat served in a rich red sauce
Sofrito - veal, garlic, parsley and vinegar…

Facts about Corfu:

Fish Market…

Corfu Cake Shop…

Eating Out on Corfu

One of the most important parts of any Greek Island holiday, and on Corfu it is also key, is the enjoying of traditional Greek food and wine! The Island of Corfu's Tavernas will not disappoint. Modern Corfiot food is fresh and exciting and thankfully long gone is the soggy Mousaka served with chips! Nowadays you will find great food at Corfu's tavernas. Since the introduction of the Euro, emphasis has been to keep prices down and quality up. Food is more expensive than the days of the drachma, but Corfu still offers excellent value for money as a holiday destination. **Where to Eat:** Around the back streets of Corfu you will find a host of kebab shops, serving pita bread crammed with meat, sauce and salad, Greek style. Authentic Greek kebabs make a great walking snack and are very affordable, although for fine dining, the restaurants within Corfu Town itself are hard to beat…

Facts about Corfu:

Eating Out on Corfu

When in Corfu Town start by taking a stroll around the Plateia Dimarchiou (Town Hall Square) and in particular, around the Kapodistriou and Guilford areas, where restaurants are at their most abundant. Alternatively, head on down to Corfu Town's Liston, have a coffee at one of the many cafes with outdoor seating, sit back and enjoy some serious people watching. Holidays on Corfu, some would say, are all about food and wine! Eating to Greeks is a way of life itself and you should always find time for a coffee or to enjoy some of the local wine. Eating is the time for Greek families to get together and socialize. The traditional highlight of the week is Sunday lunch which is a long drawn out affair that often lasts for many hours…

Facts about Corfu:

Shopping on Corfu

Holiday makers staying on the Island of Corfu are likely to want to take back home a souvenir of their Ionian holiday, and on the Island there are plenty of shopping opportunities here to do just that. Some of the most popular souvenirs on Corfu include the very tasty local honey, leather goods, and also the Island's very own olive oil. Those shopping for honey will find the best on offer is generally to be found within Kythira, while if olive oil is on your shopping list, then Paxi is the place for you. Many shops around both Paxi and Corfu Town have become well known for their handcrafted items, many of which are often carved in extraordinary detail and made from local olive wood, including items such as toys, ornaments and beautiful salad bowls…

Facts about Corfu:

Shopping on Corfu

Other gift ideas to check out when shopping in Corfu Town is some of the Island's rather famous 'mandolato' nougat, its 'tagari' woollen bags, and it's rather flavoursome kumquat liqueur. Many of the women living in villages around the Island make lace and embroidered linens, using the same traditional methods that have been used for decades. The best of these can be found in the mountain villages, rather than in the main tourist resorts. So now that we have experienced some of the treats the Island of Corfu has to offer the visitor we will, in the next chapter, take a relaxed wander around the capital of the Island Corfu Town…

Corfu Town

Kerkyra or Corfu Town, is the capital of Corfu. The Town of Corfu has much in common with Venice, Naples, France and England. The town is a historic maze of narrow streets dominated by a 16th century fortress. Around every corner of the Town you will find a chapel, old mansion or secret garden square. The café at the Liston which was built by the French in the same style as those in Rue de Rivoli, Paris; is probably the best place to 'people watch' while enjoying a Ginger beer or cup of coffee on the Island. The Island was left, by the British, the game of cricket, which is played on the pitch opposite the Liston and attracts large crowds…

Corfu Town:

In Corfu Town the narrow streets radiating away from the Liston, houses small shops of every type but dominated by 'gold shops'. Corfiot craftsmen excel at designing and making Greek jewellery in gold and this coupled with competitive prices may tempt you to buy. While you are amongst the hustle and bustle of the Town, look out for those shops and stalls selling local produce such as wild honey, fig cakes and handmade lace. The most famous church on Corfu, and the most visited, is Saint Spiridon's Church, home to the Island's patron 'mummified' saint. It is just behind the Liston in the very heart of Corfu Town…

Corfu Town:

Corfu Town is very central to life on the Island, and its Old Town district has a Venetian character, with winding cobblestone streets and sea views stretching as far as the Bay of Garitsa. Near to Corfu Town's Venetian Citadel, the Ano Plateia and Kato Plateia (Upper and Lower Squares) are surrounded by quality restaurants, tavernas and shops and there are a number of open-air events staged in the squares every year…

Corfu Town:

The northern part of Corfu Town is where the historical Old Town district can be found between the New Fortress (Neo Frourio) and the Spianada. On the eastern side of Corfu Town you will find the Old Fortress (Palaio Frourio), which is located next to the seafront and is surrounded by a moat. The southern side of Corfu Town is home to the New Town district, where the majority of retail shops and modern services can be found. There is no actual official tourist office in the town, although a tourist kiosk often operates on the Plateia San Rocco and provides maps and brochures in the summer. Maps that feature the entire Island are generally available to visitors at their hotels, free of charge so there is no excuses for getting lost. After all of the heat, dust and congestion of wandering around Corfu Town it is now time for us to head off to the Islands beaches for a bit of sunbathing and a cool dip into the lovely blue clear clean seawater in the next chapter…

The A - Z of Corfu Beaches

When it comes to glorious soft stretches of sand the Island of Corfu certainly comes with some of the finest and most alluring beaches imaginable, ranked amongst the best that the Ionian Islands have to offer. The beaches on Corfu vary greatly in size, popularity and appearance, with many summer holiday makers favoring the larger resorts of Almyros, Benitses, Ipsos (Ypsos) and Kassiopi, where facilities are extensive and accommodation is conveniently located close to the beaches.

The Main Holiday Resorts and Beaches on Corfu

Acharavi - Agni - Arilas – Avlaki – Barbati – Benitsas – Dasssia – Ermones - Saint Georgios (North and South) – Glyfada - Agios Gordios – Gouvia – Ipsos – Kalami – Kaminaki – Kassiopi – Kavos – Kerrasia – Kontokali – Messonghi -Agios Nikolas – Nissaki – Paleokastritsa - Pelekas, - Roda – Sidari - Agios (Saint) Stephanos (NE) - Agios (Saint) Stephanos (NW)

To many people the Greek Islands mean beautiful sandy beaches. The Island of Corfu is no exception as it has many varied beaches to choose from and enjoy. The beaches can be either sandy, pebbly, busy, quiet or be in a hidden rocky cove. If laying on sandy beaches is an important part of your holiday, then Corfu is just the place for you…

The A - Z of Corfu Beaches:

Sidari...

Pelekas...

Agios Georgios Beach is one of the Island's longest and most appealing sandy beaches. It is on the western side of Corfu. Many of the best resorts can be found on the western coast, such as **Pelekas Beach**, which is another extremely good holiday choice and is known locally as 'Kontogialos'. Visitors often choose Pelekas to stay in because of its extensive choice of water sports, with water skiing being a popular pastime here. On the northern shores of Corfu is the resort of **Sidari Beach**. The beach is really popular with couples and families alike as it offers peaceful coves and magical natural scenery…

The A – Z of Corfu Beaches:

Acharavi Beach

Is situated around 40 km / 25 miles from Corfu Town and is on the Island's far northerly tip. There is much more to Acharavi than first appears, with good facilities including various eateries and shops. This stretch of sand is close to Roda and around 3 km / 2 miles in length…

The A – Z of Corfu Beaches:

Agios Georgios Beach

Is a rather isolated spot and certainly one of the Island's most attractive beaches. Agios Georgios is sited some 30 km / 19 miles from Corfu Town, which stands directly to the north. It is worth coming here to see the wonderful rock formations alone. The beach here is very popular with visitors to the Island and offers soft sand. The pretty village of Sinrades is nearby and worth a visit…

The A – Z of Corfu Beaches:

Agios Stefanos Beach

The beach is a good distance from Corfu Town, which is to be found just over 44 km / 27 miles to the east of Town. Agios Stefanos is ideal for families and widely regarded to be one of the Island's safest coastal spots. This sandy beach is very much gaining popularity with tourists and becomes more and more developed every year…

The A – Z of Corfu Beaches:

Almyros Beach

Is a very lengthy expanse of sand and actually stretches for a staggering 8 km or 5 miles in total. The central part of Almyros features a highly developed tourist resort with lots of big hotel complexes and bars. This is a good place to come for water sports, since here you are able to water ski, windsurf, hire pedalos and even try your hand at parasailing high above the coastline of the Island of Corfu…

The A – Z of Corfu Beaches:

Arilas Beach

The beach is around 35 km / 22 miles to the north of Corfu Town. Arilas is a nice long sandy beach that is very family friendly and is near to Agios Stefanos. A number of gift shops are close by should you want to write a postcard whilst you sunbathe or you could just sit back and relax…

The A – Z of Corfu Beaches:

Astrakeri Beach

Astrakeri is one of the region's most popular resort beaches. It is reasonably quiet and undeveloped. Astrakeri has lush exotic vegetation, which includes lots of olive trees and tropical shrubs as a backdrop to the beach…

The A – Z of Corfu Beaches:

Barbati Beach

Barbati beach is around 20 km / 12 miles to the north of Corfu Town and near to Pyrgi. Barbati boasts a spotless beachfront and has deservedly been awarded an EU Blue Flag in recent years all of which makes this a very popular beach with holidaymakers indeed…

The A – Z of Corfu Beaches:

Bataria-Kassiopi Beach

Bataria beach is situated just 20 km / 12 miles to the north of Corfu Town. The backdrop of Mount Pantokrator is quite splendid and the slopes are brimming with mature olive plantations and citrus trees…

The A – Z of Corfu Beaches:

Benitses Beach

Benitses beach is on the Island's southerly coast and has one pebbly beach that is not to be overlooked by visitors. Benitses is outstanding and is extremely successful in its role as a leading resort. There are lots of lively night spots here, where you can enjoy live music and an unmistakable Greek atmosphere. We have stayed at the hotel featured above which is very close to this resort in the past and enjoyed the lively atmosphere very much…

The A – Z of Corfu Beaches:

Boukari Beach

Boukari beach is a very tranquil resort known for its seafood restaurants and long expanse of small pebbled beach. Boukari is never crowded and can be found 25 km / 16 miles to the south of Corfu Town…

The A – Z of Corfu Beaches:

Canal d'Amour Beach

Canal d'Amour beach is some 34 km / 21 miles to the north of Corfu Town. The resort of Sidari lies directly east of Canal d'Amour beach. The beach has become famous with its visitors for its awesome and beautiful coves…

The A – Z of Corfu Beaches:

Dassia Beach

Dassia beach can to be found on the eastern side of Corfu, overlooking Albania and is regularly overflowing with tourists in the summer. Dassia is mainly a pebbly beach next to a long line of hotels. Our very good friends Corri and Roy have stayed in this resort and had a great holiday…

The A – Z of Corfu Beaches:

Ermones Beach

Ermones beach is on the western side of the Island, opposite Kerkyra and near to the village of Ermones. The beachfront is backed by a steep cliff face, which is actually connected to a hotel by a scenic cable car ride, affording superb views of the surrounding area…

The A – Z of Corfu Beaches:

Gialiskari Beach

Gialiskari beach can be found lying some 15 km / 9 miles to the south-west of Corfu Town and next to the village of Sinarades. Gialiskari is one of the area's best beaches for water sports and provides a range of good facilities and is therefore popular with Island visitors…

The A – Z of Corfu Beaches:

Glyfada Beach

If you are looking for a stunning sandy beach then probably this beach is the finest the Island has to offer. Glyfada should be on your list of places to consider for your next holiday. There are several bars and tavernas around Glyfada beach as well as the usual hotels and apartments. Glyfada beach is on the western coastline of the Island of Corfu and close to Pelekas. Glyfada really is amongst the Island's most beautiful beaches and is known for its 'Blue Flag' award for cleanliness. The beachfront is a good place for playing volleyball, while water sports facilities include water skiing, jet-skiing and pedalo-type boats. All in all a very good bucket and spade resort…

The A – Z of Corfu Beaches:

Gouvia Beach

Gouvia beach is located on the northern side of Corfu Town and also relatively near to Dassia and Pyrgi. If you are driving to this resort, you will most likely need to actually park on the adjacent road away from the beach front as there is limited access nearer to the seafront…

The A – Z of Corfu Beaches:

Halikounas Beach

Halikounas beach has a very lengthy stretch of sand and is close to Agios Matheos village and roughly 24 km / 15 miles from Corfu Town, which stands directly to the north…

The A – Z of Corfu Beaches:

Imerolias Beach

Imerolias beach is close to the village of Sidari and some 33 km / 21 miles to the north of Corfu Town…

The A – Z of Corfu Beaches:

Ipsos Beach (Ypsos)

Ipsos beach enjoys a scenic easterly location, next to the village of Ypsos. This really is perhaps rather too overdeveloped and touristy for some. The resort is overflowing with burger bars, gift shops and lots of holiday makers, who come here to parasail and enjoy zooming around on inflatable banana boat rides. This resort is not for the faint heart…

The A – Z of Corfu Beaches:

Kalamionas Beach

Kalamionas beach is close to the resort of Sidari and is around 30 km / 19 miles from Corfu Town, which is situated to the south…

The A – Z of Corfu Beaches:

Kalami Beach

Kalami beach is a pebbly stretch of beach which is really more of a bay than an actual beach. Visitors come here for the great snorkeling and beautiful scenery. Close by is a large holiday complex. Interestingly, Kalami has a strong connection with conversationalist Gerald Durrell and his family, who actually once lived in this part of the Island of Corfu. There are a number of other good sandy beaches in close proximity to Kalami Beach…

The A – Z of Corfu Beaches:

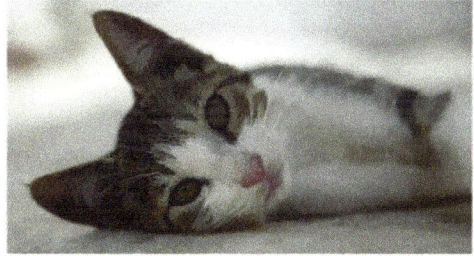

Kaminaki Beach and Village

Kaminaki beach enjoys a very appealing setting alongside steep slopes brimming with olive trees. The beachfront here is comprised mainly of pebbles and has the advantage of being very secluded. Children will always enjoy paddling in the sea here. If you hire a boat, then be sure to explore all of the coves and natural inlets along the coast nearby. Kaminaki Beach features its own small grocery store should you fancy an impromptu picnic, although a couple of tavernas are also close by. Kaminaki is one of Corfu's best kept secrets. It is a tiny beach-fronted village, tucked away amongst the olive groves. The bay is a beautiful well-kept secret with sparkling white pebbles and a turquoise water gently lapping onto the beach. It is almost a dream and probably the one that many of us have when we picture a small Greek holiday destination. One Taverna sits right on the beach, while another sits up high on the rocks overlooking the bay. The atmosphere is friendly and is not dissimilar to other smaller coastal resorts in the immediate area. To-date the beach and bay is quiet and relatively untouched by tourism…

The A – Z of Corfu Beaches:

Kanoni Beach

Kanoni beach is around 33 km / 21 miles directly north of Corfu Town and is one of the Island's more trendy spots. Lots of hotels and similar accommodation can be found close by and around the Sidari area in general…

The A – Z of Corfu Beaches:

Kassiopi Village and Beach

Kassiopi village and beach is a major tourist resort, with a pebbly beachfront. We have had a great two weeks holiday in this resort in the past which we enjoyed very much. The resort is very commercial however, there seems to be a successful compromise and in most places it is not at all tacky or overdone. Watch out for the sea urchins, which often seem to lurk around the rocks in the sea. They really do hurt a lot if you fall foul of them so be careful…

The A – Z of Corfu Beaches:

Kerasia Beach

Kerasia beach is sited on the far north-easterly side of Corfu and alongside the resort of Plagia. Kerasia features some rather impressive views across the sea to Albania. There are always plenty of sunbeds and umbrellas available for hire here. The water is fairly shallow for the first few metres, becoming quite deep a little further out and therefore ideal for swimmers. Countless olive trees and pine trees surround the beachfront. Prince Charles is known to come here from time to time, staying on a nearby estate with friends…

The A – Z of Corfu Beaches:

Kouloura Beach

Kouloura beach is found on the north-eastern side of the Island, close to Kalami and also Vigla. The stretch of sand here is really rather narrow and small, although the undeveloped setting is just lovely. There are lots of interesting rocky coves around Kouloura, which are just begging to be investigated and explored by visitors…

The A – Z of Corfu Beaches:

Krouzeri Beach

Krouzeri beach is a truly spectacular spot awarded the EU Blue Flag for its cleanliness and excellent facilities. Krouzeri can be found on the Island some 25 km / 16 miles to the north of Corfu Town. Visitors can expect to see lots of colourful flowers, historic groves of olive trees and small white pebbles on the beach. The surrounding seawater seem to shimmer and exude a rich emerald colour and is lovely to swim in…

The A – Z of Corfu Beaches:

Liapades Beach

Liapades beach is a very natural and undeveloped spot approximately 20 km / 12 miles from Corfu Town and located to the north-west. Liapades beach is bounded by some rather picturesque mountain slopes and is very near to the really beautiful resort of Paleokastritsa…

The A – Z of Corfu Beaches:

Marathias Beach

Marathias beach is around 200 metres long and some 10 metres deep and covered with sunbeds and umbrellas. The facilities at Marathias are very good and it is even possible to hire bicycles here. There are several notable hotels close by and due to its small size sunbathing space can sometimes be at a premium on the beach…

The A – Z of Corfu Beaches:

Messonghi Beach

Messonghi beach is directly 20 km - 12 miles to the south of Corfu Town. Messonghi is great for families with young children and also offers a wide choice of fun water sports activities. So children should remember to take their bucket and spade with them for hours of fun on the beach…

The A – Z of Corfu Beaches:

Myrtiotissa Beach

Myrtiotissa beach is situated on the western coastline of the Island of Corfu and directly beneath the Monastery of Myrtiotissa, near to Pelekas and is close to a number of very good vineyards. The views around Myrtiotissa beach are awesome and you may possibly encounter some naturist if you come here so be advised…

The A – Z of Corfu Beaches:

Nissaki Island

Nissaki means Little Island and hundreds of years ago that is what it was. On top of the Island, now stands a Taverna. In years past, the local people worked on this Island, shaping stones and local rocks bought to them by boat. The stones were used for building work. After many years of the discarded stone chipping's falling into the sea they formed a ramp and eventually joined the Island to the mainland of Corfu. Now there is a narrow road that runs between the old Island where the Taverna stands and the mainland. Nissaki has a small beach and is extremely pretty. The beach is a small horseshoe shape with fine pebbles, offering excellent swimming, although it can become a little crowded when day trip boats arrive for lunch…

The A – Z of Corfu Beaches:

Paleokastritsa Beach

Paleokastritsa beach is a very pretty spot famed for its extreme natural beauty and stunning rocky coves. Islanders like to believe the romantic story that Paleokastritsa was once home to the palace of King Alcinous. King Alcinous was, in Greek mythology, a son of Nausithous, or of Phaeax, and father of Nausicaa, Halius, Clytoneus and Laodamas with Arete. His name literally means "mighty mind". We spent several happy days relaxing on the beautiful beaches here and wandering around the countryside close by. It was truly wonderful…

The A – Z of Corfu Beaches:

Pelekas Beach (Kontogialos)

Pelekas beach enjoys a scenic westerly location, in close proximity to Pelekas village, which is well worth exploring if you have the time. This is a highly recommended sunny spot for tourists to frequent. Kontogialos is lined by a good variety of Greek-style tavernas and bars, while those looking to indulge in water sports will find they can water ski, hire motorboats and do much, much more besides on this beach…

The A – Z of Corfu Beaches:

Perama Beach

Perama beach is found on the Island's easterly shore, with charming sandy connected coves that are located alongside the lively town of Benitses. Perama is amongst the most scenic beaches in the area and worth having a lazy day relaxing on…

The A – Z of Corfu Beaches:

Pipitos Beach

Pipitos beach is situated around 37 km - 23 miles to the north of Corfu Town and once again it is close to the resort of Sidari…

The A – Z of Corfu Beaches:

Roda Beach

Roda beach can be found some 35 km - 22 miles to the north of Corfu Town and is alongside a scenic fishing harbour. Roda is very much an up-and-coming tourist resort, with lots of palm trees and clear shallow seawater making it perfect for families holidaying with young children. This is another must bring your bucket and spade resort…

The A – Z of Corfu Beaches:

Sidari Beach

Sidari beach is one of the most famous beaches on the northern side of the Island and simply a must-see for everyone who comes to the Island. We had a great day swimming and sunbathing in the many coves at Sidari. This resort is around 30 km - 19 miles from Corfu Town and home to some wonderfully eroded and shaped rocks (a must see), which appear almost like sculptures that have been shaped by nature. There are lots of small and secluded coves in the immediate area, where you can swim, sunbathe or simply lay back and just relax and enjoy the wonderful views…

The A – Z of Corfu Beaches:

Yaliskari Beach

Yaliskari beach is backed by mature pine trees and boasting a fine sandy beach. Yaliskari is located on Corfu's western coast and whilst it may not be one of the biggest beaches on the Island, it does have a lot of appeal and good facilities, which include snack bars, pedalos and a nearby car park. In the next chapter we will be looking at some of these beaches again, in more detail, so if you are ready let us take a more leisurely stroll along some of the best beaches on the Island of Corfu…

The Best Beaches on Corfu

Paleokastritsa

Paleokastritsa is arguably the most famous picturesque village on the Island of Corfu and is located 25 km northwest of Corfu Town. The word *Paleokastritsa* literally means old fortress, witnessing the existence of such a castle on the rocky hill where now stands the Monastery of the Virgin. The village of Paleokastritsa offers a plethora of local tavernas overlooking the blue bay with its six sandy and pebbled beaches which are scattered all around the area. These beaches are surrounded by olive tree forests creating a dramatic yet beautiful backdrop. This cosmopolitan resort stretches along a coastal road around stunning bays and a picturesque harbour where the excursion boats depart for the nearby and isolated beaches. The settlement has managed to retain its traditional Greek charm and character. Today it is considered one of the main tourist attractions on the Island of Corfu. It has a great number of hotels, bars and restaurants. At the end of the road, right after the main harbour and on a hill is the Monastery of the Virgin that dominates the village. The monastery has an interesting collection of post Byzantine icons, books and other objects. The main beach of Paleokastritsa is quite small but is extremely well known for its cold seawater and delightful environment. It is considered to be one of the best beaches on the Greek Islands. It is, as a result, surrounded by a lot of bars and taverns. The area also offers some excellent sea views…

The Best Beaches on Corfu:

Agios Gordios

Agios Gordios is one of the most popular beaches on the Island of Corfu. It took its name from the church of Agios Gordios located literally on the seashore, at the centre of the beach. The beautiful cove is nestled amongst the lush green mountain surrounded by olive tree forests, vineyards and impressive rocks. To reach the beach of Agios Gordios you pass through a beautiful road full of vineyards and high olive trees. Once on the beach the crystalline seawater is ideal for a refreshing swim while water sports equipment is also available for both children and adults. During the day, the beach is quite noisy as the children enjoy playing in the waves and making sand castles. The beach is bordered by the impressive Ortholithi, a huge rock emerging from the sea. The resort with its beautiful landscape and beach Agios Gordios offers an ideal summer holiday destination…

The Best Beaches on Corfu:

Glyfada Beach

Glyfada beach is one of the most popular beaches on the Island of Corfu. Glyfada is located 16 km west of Corfu Town. It has been awarded the Blue Flag for its crystal clear seawater while the large soft golden sand of the beach is surrounded by trees that cover the cliffs and the imposing rocky formations. The beach offers a wide variety of beach facilities like sunbeds and umbrellas, water sports facilities, shops and tavernas. Glyfada attracts mostly the young crowd and it is usually very noisy. Glyfada has one of the best examples of the Island's golden sandy beaches…

The Best Beaches on Corfu:

Myrtiotissa Beach

Myrtiotissa is a sandy paradise of a beach that is surrounded by a landscape of lush green cliffs and crystalline clear seawater. The beach was a favourite of the English writer Lawrence Durrell. He said that it was the *loveliest beach in the world* for its dramatic and stunning surroundings that attract thousands of visitors every year. Myrtiotissa is one of the most popular beaches on Corfu. It owes its name to the beautiful Monastery of Myrtiotissa which stands on the slopes of the surrounding lush green mountain, above the sea. This idyllic beach retains its unspoiled character. People often come to the beach on the local bus from Corfu Town. When you reach Myrtiotissa you will have to follow a long path that leads directly to the beach. Those who want to visit the monastery will have to take the road that goes uphill from the main road. After 300 meters walk you will see the monastery high above which has great views of the surrounding countryside and sea…

The Best Beaches on Corfu:

Nissaki Beach

Nissaki is amongst the most beautiful beaches on the Island of Corfu. It has a lovely sandy shore surrounded by rock formations and is located between the villages of Barbati and Kassiopi, 22 km north of Corfu Town. The small beach at Nissaki which is situated well away from the road offers only a few tourist facilities. Nissaki bay is protected from the strong winds, nevertheless the water gets gradually deeper the further you swim out. The beach is a great place for families while the rocks on either side of the beach are a good place to explore. The seawater is so clear and clean here that you can see the rich marine life in the beautiful underwater landscape clearly. Next to the beach is a small quaint port where fishing boats are moored. The beach is surrounded by good tavernas serving fresh seafood and other local delicacies…

The Best Beaches on Corfu:

Canal d'Amour (Channel of Love)

The village of Sidari is well known as being one of the best tourist resorts on Corfu and is located 36 km from Corfu Town. The village is surrounded by a charming landscape full of lush green forests. Nearby, to the west is the famous Channel of Love (known as Canal d' Amour) an idyllic area with unique rock formations that form a series of wonderful coves and canals. We spent several days here. The rocks run in bands of different shades of yellow and have lots of greenery on the top. The stunning coves are reach by going down one of the several paths and steps that lead down to them from the village. With its beautiful crystalline seawater, the Channel of Love is one of the most unique spots on Corfu. According to local tradition couples who swim through the narrow canal here will get married soon. As we were already married Susie and I did not benefit from our swims around the coves in this way. Visiting the beach is not recommended on a windy day…

The Best Beaches on Corfu:

Agios Georgios Pagon Beach

Down a winding, scenic and beautiful road, about 40 km northwest of the Town of Corfu, lies the beautiful resort of Agios Georgios Pagon which is set in the mouth of a beautiful valley, this resort has a perfect beach which is ideal for families as it provides endless fun for the children and a peaceful relaxing day for the adults. The beach has been awarded a Blue Flag for its crystal clear seawater and fantastic environment. The beach consists of soft golden sand mixed with some large shiny pebbles. There are plenty of umbrellas and sunbeds provided for hire and the beach is surrounded by beautiful cypress trees that grow along the edge of the bay. Agios Georgios beach is a natural oasis. The nearby cliffs and historic villages are ideal destinations for hiking. The restaurants and tavernas offer good quality local food with the added bonus of perfect sunset views…

The Best Beaches on Corfu:

Issos Beach

Issos is a beautiful beach located 35 km south of Corfu Town. The seemingly endless seashore with its unique sand dunes and crystalline seawater offers an ideal holiday destination for families. Rich flora divides the seashore from the most important wetland found on Corfu, the Korission Lake. This idyllic area is definitely one of the best places to visit on the Island of Corfu. Along the sandy beach lie plenty of tourist facilities and various beach equipment. There is a lifeguard tower and a water-sports centre on the beach. Issos beach is affected by the strong winds that often blow in this part of the Island which makes it one of the best place for windsurfing and kitesurfing on the Island. The nearby lush green forest and the lake make this a unique spot for hiking while the high sand dunes offer excellent sunset views. Close to the beach are some good bars and fine tavernas…

The Best Beaches on Corfu:

Kalami Beach

Kalami beach is considered to be one of Corfu's most picturesque spots located 30 km from the main Town. The main beach is composed of white shiny pebbles and clear turquoise seawater. Kalami beach is world famous for its unspoiled landscape that inspired the English author Lawrence Durrell to write his novel *Prospero's cell*. The beach has been awarded a Blue Flag for its cleanness and it offers a wide variety of water sports activities for a fun packed family holiday. Sunbeds and umbrellas are available to hire for a comfortable day on the beach. The beach is surrounded by lush vegetation and forests. Right behind Kalami beach the holiday accommodation built amongst the trees provide an ideal environment for a peaceful and relaxing holiday…

The Best Beaches on Corfu:

Agios Stefanos Beach

Agios Stefanos is a long sandy beach in the region of Avliotes, 40 km North West of Corfu Town. Surrounded by lush greenery, this lovely beach has crystal clear seawater and soft golden sand. Delicious food is served at the tavernas that line the beach. This is a quiet and calm place ideal for families and people who want to just relax. At the end of the beach, there is a small marina that has local fishing boats and private yachts bobbing up and down in it all day long…

The Best Beaches on Corfu:

Imerolias Beach Kassiopi

The beach of Imerolias Kassiopi, is ideally located on the western side of Kassiopi village and 36 km north-eastern of Corfu Town. Near Kassiopi, one of the most popular resorts with convenient facilities and picturesque spots is the pebbled beach of Imerolias which is usually pleasantly quiet and easily accessed. The beach is distinguished by its turquoise seawater in an unspoiled setting…

The Best Beaches on Corfu:

Barbati Beach

The beautiful coastal settlement of Barbati is situated 17 km north of Corfu Town. The beach lies around a natural bay. It is one of the most impressive beaches on the Island of Corfu. It is surrounded by lush green forests and hills. The beach is very inviting and is lapped by crystalline clear seawater and has white shiny pebbles all over it. The beach has plenty of sunbeds, umbrellas and watersports facilities. Small tour boats are available to hire for a short and exciting trip to the many nearby coves and bays. Tavernas and bars serving delicious Corfiot flavours and cold drinks are close by the beach…

The Best Beaches on Corfu:

Ermones Beach

Ermones is a beautiful beach located 18 km west of Corfu Town. The beach consists of sand and pebbles, ideal for all tastes and has crystal clear seawater cascading onto its beach. Ermones beach is a favourite with lovers of diving and experienced swimmers. A unique diving centre operates from the beach offering the visitor a really fascinating underwater experience. The beach is boarded by hills and vegetation this unique combination attracts many return visitors every year. Sunbeds and umbrellas are for hire on the beach. A walk along the shore leads to several smaller bays which are ideal for total privacy. Good quality tavernas are found in the wider area. Ermones is a nice alternative if you want a quiet and pleasant holiday. Several hotels are located right behind the bay itself…

The Best Beaches on Corfu:

Agios Georgios Argyradon Beach

Agios Georgios Argyradon is a small, sandy beach located 32 km south of Corfu Town and 8 km south of Messonghi. The beautiful settlement that lies around the beach is not over developed and is known for the natural beauty of its landscape. The sandy beach has sunbeds and umbrellas but its main attraction is its tranquil and beautiful environment. It has naturally been awarded a Blue Flag for its cleanness…

The Best Beaches on Corfu:

Dassia Beach

Dassia is a popular resort located between the villages of Gouvia and Ipsos, 13 km from Corfu Town. It has a friendly and cosmopolitan atmosphere. Dassia has become one of the most inviting places to spend a relaxing holiday on Corfu and our friends Corri and Roy have recently spent a great two weeks there doing just that. Right in front of the village is a magnificent narrow beach that stretches for a couple of kilometres. It consist of sand and pebbles with two rows of sunbeds and umbrellas for those who want to enjoy a comfortable time sunbathing. Dassia beach is quite flat with no sand dunes offering a perfect view to the Albanian coast. At the centre of the beach there is a platform where people can dive into the crystalline clear seawater. This beach can be quite lively and busy in the summer months. Trees at the back of the beach provide some nice natural shade. Small tour boats are also available to hire for a short trip to the nearby beaches. A walk along the beach leads to several smaller bays which are ideal for total privacy. The beach also offers a fascinating view of the Monastery of Pantokrator…

The Best Beaches on Corfu:

Halikounas Beach

Halikounas beach is ideally located 25 km south west of Corfu Town. The sandy beach that stretches for more than 3 km is considered to be one of the most beautiful coastal areas in the Ionian complex of Islands. Halikounas is a nice alternative for peaceful holidays with sand dunes and wonderful crystalline seawater which guarantee a fun swimming experience especially for the children. Halikounas is ideal for those who love water sports as well. A road separates the beach from the famous Lake Korission, one of the main attractions of the area which is the home of numerous endangered bird species. It is nestled in the middle of green rolling hills that have verdant olive groves, citrus orchards and beautiful vineyards. There are many modern amenities such as hotels, restaurants, tavernas and bars in the area. From Halikounas, you have a perfect view to the ancient monastery perched on the top of Mount Agios Mattheos. The beach is located 5 km from the popular resort of Agios Georgios…

The Best Beaches on Corfu:

Liapades Beach

The picturesque beach of Liapades is tucked away on the northern coast of Corfu, about 30 km from the main Town. The surrounding area of Liapades is filled with vineyards, lush greenery and verdant fields. The area is sparsely populated and is unique for its Ionian architecture. A must indulge in activity on Liapades beach is that of snorkeling which is great due to the crystal clear seawater and the fascinating marine life that can be found just offshore. There are a few tourist facilities to be found on the pebbled shore while the sea is ideal for numerous watersports. You can also have the option of hiring a speed boat and embarking on a tour of the many uninhabited beaches that are located nearby…

The Best Beaches on Corfu:

Peroulades Beach

Peroulades is a narrow beach encircled by imposing hills. It is located 36 km northwest of Corfu Town and is considered to be one of the most beautiful spots to be found anywhere on the Island. The beach has perpendicular rocky cliffs which are rather difficult to reach, via a very steep path. This beach is impeccably maintained and rather well organized. From the small sandy beach you can enjoy breathtaking sunset views. Tavernas, bars and a nice choice of accommodation lie around the bay…

The Best Beaches on Corfu:

Arilas Beach

The long sandy beach of Arilas lies in front of a beautiful village located 40 km from Corfu Town. The beach is surrounded by lush forests and vast olive groves. The beach that stretches for about 2 km is a favourite destination for families and for people who seek a peaceful and restful holiday. It is an attractive resort, ideal for safe swimming as the seawater is shallow and very clean, perfect for the children. Hire a boat and you can visit the two nearby deserted islets of Diaplos and Mathraki. Do not forget to visit the picturesque village of Afionas nearby to enjoy spectacular sunsets…

The Best Beaches on Corfu:

Bataria Beach

Bataria is a beautiful beach in Kassiopi, located 37 km from Corfu Town. Bataria is a small beach but it is loved for its wild beauty and perfect views of the Albanian mountains across the sea that make this an ideal setting for your summer holiday. Right behind the small port of Kassiopi is the magnificent cove of Bataria, an inviting area with crystal clear seawater and shiny pebbles. The beach has rough rocks and green vegetation which creates a relaxing and beautiful spot to enjoy. The pebbled shore has sunbeds and some space for those who want some privacy. Despite its close proximity to the village, Bataria keeps a low profile, away from the noisy crowds that one will find on many of the other beaches in the Kassiopi area. The beach is kept very clean and is a friendly environment which makes it an ideal place for children to play. Various accommodation, tavernas and bars can be found close by on the main street of Kassiopi village…

The Best Beaches on Corfu:

Agios Ioannis Peristeron Beach

Agios Ioannis Peristeron beach is a long sandy beach located 18 km south of Corfu Town. The surrounding area is covered by lush forests and vegetation. As this beach is situated far away from the more busy resorts on the Island it is considered to be a good beach for those who want a quiet place to relax on. It has crystal clear seawater and golden sand that is ideal for beach games. Along the beach you will find a nice choice of taverns and accommodation. The surrounding region has picturesque villages to explore and lovely coves that offer total privacy. This beach is a great place to take the children with their buckets and spades…

The Best Beaches on Corfu:

Marathias Beach

Marathias beach is a beautiful coastal resort on the southwest coast of the Island of Corfu. The beach is highly recommended by the locals for its crystal clear seawater and the golden sand on its beach. The long sandy beach surrounded by an imposing hill forest is ideal for all tastes. On the beach there are umbrellas and sunbeds for hire and the beach-side tavernas offer good quality food with beautiful panoramic views out to sea. The lovely sandy beach at Marathias extends for over 2 km…

The Best Beaches on Corfu:

Gardeno Beach

Gardeno beach is a little gem, one of Corfu's undiscovered delights located 40 km southwest of the main Town of Corfu and 5 km from the village of Lefkimmi. The long sandy beach is distinguished not only for the lush green setting but also for its tranquil atmosphere. The shallow and crystalline seawater provides a safe place for children to paddle which makes this beach an ideal place for a family holiday. A long line of cypress clad hills offer natural shade and there are sunbeds and umbrellas also available for hire on the beach. It is well worth visiting the tavernas that overlook the blue bay after a refreshing swim in the sea or a sunbathing session on Gardeno beach…

The Best Beaches on Corfu:

Agios Spiridon Beach

The beach at Agios Spiridon is one of the quietest and beautiful beaches located on the northeast coast of the Island of Corfu. Agios Spiridon is a sandy beach with crystal clear seawater that has a lush backdrop of greenery. The beach has been awarded a Blue Flag for its cleanness. The seashore is fully equipped with sunbeds, umbrellas and water sports facilities. Close by you will find numerous good restaurants, tavernas, shops and hotels. The beach is situated near the protected wetland of Antinioti Lagoon, between the tourist resorts of Kassiopi and Arachavi. Also nearby stands the beautiful monastery of Agia Ekaterini…

The Best Beaches on Corfu:

Agios Iliodoros Beach

Agios Iliodoros (or Linodoros) beach is a beautiful cape located 17 km west of Corfu Town. It lies close to the villages of Liapades and Paleokastritsa. Right below the village is the main beach covered with soft golden sand. It is surrounded by lush hills that lead directly to the edge of the water. The beach lacks facilities due to its small size, but it provides a rare natural beauty that attracts many visitors every summer. The idyllic surroundings of Agios Iliodoros is a perfect spot for the nature lovers and for those who want to enjoy some peaceful moments with their family and friends...

The Best Beaches on Corfu:

Agios Stefanos Port and Beach

Agios Stefanos is a small port for fishing boats and yachts and is close to the lovely village of Kassiopi. Located about 35 km north east of Corfu Town, Agios Stefanos is surrounded by lush greenery. It also has traditional tavernas and seaside cafeterias. Right next to the port, there is a small pebbled beach to relax on or to go for a swim from. The coastline of Agios Stefanos has some very good diving sports to enjoy…

The Best Beaches on Corfu:

Agni Beach

The beach at Agni bay is located 30 km from the main Town of Corfu and 11 km from the village of Kassiopi. The petite bay consists of shiny pebbles and a few patches of sand. There are good tavernas here that are open only during the summer season that offer breathtaking views of the Albanian coasts. Wild vegetation and pebbles encircle the beach. The bay has some jetties that offer anchorage for the boats that ply for tourist trade that leave from here. The beach slopes steeply into the sea and there are numerous jagged submerged rocks that make it unsafe and out of bounds to children. Sunbeds are provided by the tavernas on the beach. The scenic beauty of Agni beach provides visitors with a tranquil place to enjoy their holiday in. In Agni there is a diving centre offering numerous training courses that they offer to enthusiasts and amateurs alike. You can even reach Agni by local bus. Near the beach there are two tavernas serving famous Corfiot dishes and delicious seafood delicacies to enjoy…

The Best Beaches on Corfu:

Almyros Beach

Almyros beach is one of the longest beaches on Corfu and is located 45 km from the Islands main Town. It stretches for 7 km and is actually a continuation of Arachavi beach. The beach is known for its shallow seawater and the soft sand that create a perfect and safe environment for the children. This is a great beach for a bucket and spade holiday. In contrast to the cosmopolitan beach of Arachavi, Almyros offers a more peaceful setting without it lacking the basic tourist facilities like sunbeds and umbrellas. A couple of meters from the beach are some nice fish tavernas with gorgeous views out to sea as far as the Albanian coast. In the tavernas you can enjoy delicious Corfiot food and excellent seafood delicacies. There are frequent local buses that run between Almyros village and Corfu Town…

The Best Beaches on Corfu:

Alonaki Beach

Alonaki is a nice clean beach located 28 km from the main Town of Corfu. It is northeast of Korrision Lake and is ideal for swimming, with crystalline seawater set in fantastic surroundings. Alonaki beach is famous for its nudist crowds and its beauty. Tourist facilities are not available on this beach apart from a small bar serving snacks and cold drinks. The area is surrounded by large rocks and there is a small cave around the north side of the beach that makes the area even more impressive. There are also plenty of car parking space beside the beach…

The Best Beaches on Corfu:

Astrakeri Beach

Astrakeri beach is found on the northern side of Corfu, approximately 40 km from Corfu Town. It is between the tourist resorts of Sidari and Roda. This is a nice beach for swimming, especially for children due to the shallow and crystalline seawater. The long sandy shore is covered with umbrellas and sundecks and nearby there is a water sports centre. There is easy access from the beach to bars and tavernas that offer spectacular views of the bay. Astrakeri beach provides one of the best place for relaxation and tranquility on the Island of Corfu and an ideal bucket and spade location for the children…

The Best Beaches on Corfu:

Avlaki Beach

Avlaki Beach is located about 37 km to the north of Corfu Town, between the villages of Agios Stefanos and Kassiopi. Avlaki is not particularly well known, although it has a very nice, pebbly beach with crystal clear seawater. Avlaki is a quiet beach which makes it an ideal holiday destination for families. The beach has sunbeds and a few tavernas serving delicious local food. In the afternoon, a northern sea breeze blows onto the beach blowing the heat away and reducing the temperature. The beach promises a lot of scope for water sports, such as sailing and canoeing. Boats are also available for hire. Small cruise boats will take you to the nearby bays. Avlaki Beach is equipped with all the basic facilities for tourists such as showers, toilets and changing rooms. Parking facilities are provided on the opposite side of or at the end of the beach. Avlaki beach is a very tranquil destination However, you will find plenty of bars in Kassiopi, just a couple of km away…

The Best Beaches on Corfu:

Boukari Village and Beach

Boukari is a picturesque fishing village located 26 km from Corfu Town. The main beach of Boukari has a crystalline and shallow sea that provides safe swimming to all visitors and especially for children. The area is well known for its prominent location offering breathtaking views of the Island of Corfu and its lush green scenery. This beach attracts mostly families seeking a relaxing and peaceful holiday. Boukari beach is surrounded by a vast area of olive groves that provide natural shade to the visitors. The beach is relatively small with no beach facilities. There is only a bar serving drinks and snacks. The beach has a clear clean sea to swim in and a tranquil atmosphere to enjoy. In the wider area you will find a plethora of hotels and fish tavernas that the village is rightly famous for. Close to Boukari, about 3 km away is the picturesque village of Messonghi, a beautiful and ideal area for hikers. Also close by is the small fishing village of Petriti…

The Best Beaches on Corfu:

Danilia Beach

Danilia (or Dafnila) beach is a small pebbled beach located on the eastern coast of the Island of Corfu, 12 km from the main Town. The beach itself is in an excellent bay and has no tourist facilities. The beach is characterized by its unspoiled beauty and lush green setting. The seawater is usually calm and totally protected from any strong winds. There is a luxurious hotel within a short distance of the beach. The area can get very crowded and usually there are several tourist boats entering the small bay every day. The clean beach and refreshing crystal clear seawater offer the visitor the best swimming experience and a feeling of total relaxation. Nearby you will find a local taverna serving delicious Corfiot food. The closest village to Danilia beach is Dassia…

The Best Beaches on Corfu:

Gialiskari Beach

Gialiskari beach is ideally located 15 km west of Corfu Town. This beach uniquely combines a lush green setting with the blue crystalline seawater of the bay making Gialiskari beach one of the most picturesque areas on the Island of Corfu. Its tropical setting is much preferred by the visitors who come here and are always amazed by its beautiful Corfiot landscape. The beach is small yet well-organized with sunbeds and umbrellas. Water sports facilities are also available for the more adventurous types. The magnificent rocky background offers natural shade and the wider area guarantees peace and quiet. Right behind the beach several hotels and tavernas can be found…

The Best Beaches on Corfu:

Gialou Beach

Gialou beach is a long beach situated 36 km northwest of Corfu Town. It is a secluded location surrounded by steep cliffs and lush vegetation. The beach is covered with sand and small pebbles that reach right down to the seawater. The seawater is clean, clear but only shallow for the first 2 meters then it gets deep very quickly. The beach has a rocky background and is a good reference point for when out swimming. Due to its secluded location, the beach receives only a few visitors who love its peaceful atmosphere, therefore this is an ideal spot for those who like total privacy. Gialou beach is easily accessed from the main coast road…

The Best Beaches on Corfu:

Glyko Beach

Glyko beach is one of the lesser known beaches on the Island of Corfu. Glyko is located 18 km from the main Town, very close to Liapades village and a couple of kilometres away from Paleokastritsa. Glyko beach is in a small cove surrounded by rough rocks. The beach is best known for its wild beauty and for being in a unique unspoiled setting. The beach is not recommended for children. The rough terrain doesn't allow any facilities therefore those adults who want to enjoy total privacy on Glyko beach can relax on the rocks under the warm sun. The beach area can be accessed through a footpath from Liapades village. You can also visit the nearby secluded beach of Rovinia also located close to Paleokastritsa…

The Best Beaches on Corfu:

Kalamaki Beach

Kalamaki beach also known as Apraos, is a calm beach located 37 km northwest of Corfu Town, between the fishing village of Kassiopi and the beach of Agios Spiridon. The calm crystal seawater and the white sand make this beach an ideal spot for peaceful family holidays. The area close to the beach is quite well-developed offering tourist facilities for a comfortable sunbathing experience. There are also several tavernas to visit after you have had a refreshing swim in the seawater off of Kalamaki beach. Boats leaving off the beach offer short trips to nearby isolated bays…

The Best Beaches on Corfu:

Kalamionas Beach Kassiopi

Kalamionas beach is one of the most attractive beaches in Kassiopi which is located 35 km north east of Corfu Town. It is a clean beach with crystalline seawater and soft sand, only 300 metres from the centre of Kassiopi. On Kalamionas beach there are numerous facilities available and plenty of accommodation options close by to suit all tastes. Kassiopi is considered a cosmopolitan place and is very busy during the summer season. Kalamionas beach is a beautiful spot for diving and swimming. Visitors are guaranteed a relaxing and memorable stay here as we found out when we stayed here…

The Best Beaches on Corfu:

Kanoni Beach Kassiopi

Kanoni beach is a beautiful beach located 35 km from the main Town of Corfu. The beach is actually a rocky cove easily accessed within a five minute walk from the main settlement of Kassiopi. It is one of Corfu's most attractive areas characterized by the crystal clear seawater and the fantastic beauty of the surrounding countryside. The little picturesque beach has few tourist facilities except for a few sunbeds and umbrellas. Just in case you do not want to be at the centre of attention, you can also relax on the rocks nearby under the warm sun. The beach can seem a bit isolated despite its close proximity to the popular resort. The rough landscape is definitely dangerous for children while it makes an ideal spot for those adults who want to enjoy total privacy during the high season…

The Best Beaches on Corfu:

Kanouli Beach

Kanouli beach is a peaceful sandy beach located 22 km away from the main Town of Corfu. Unfortunately there are no tourist facilities and very few tavernas in the surrounding area however, Kanouli beach makes an ideal spot for a relaxing day on the beach. The area does however, provide a home for many rare bird species which can be found nearby at the nature reserve at Lake Korission. The beach is very quiet and has crystal clear seawater that is excellent for swimming, snorkeling and diving. Kanouli beach is actually a continuation of Halikounas beach that is surrounded by a vast area of olive groves and trees. Some impressive rock formations add to the spectacular surroundings…

The Best Beaches on Corfu:

Kavos Beach

Kavos beach is the most popular resort in southern Corfu and a busy place with people on the beach from the early morning right up until late afternoon and into the evening. Located approximately 50 km south of Corfu Town, Kavos beach is regarded as one of the most frequented and busy beaches on the Island. The large beach is covered with golden sand and it is fully equipped with umbrellas and sunbeds. The beach is totally safe for children due to its clean and shallow seawater and therefore, great for sand castle making so bring your bucket and spade. Around Kavos beach, there are many snack bars, beach bars, tavernas, hotels and shops. Local buses connect Kavos with Corfu Town. At night, this resort turns into a popular nightlife spot and many venues stay open until the early hours. This is not a resort for the faint hearted…

The Best Beaches on Corfu:

Kerasia Beach

Kerasia beach is one of the most picturesque and beautiful beaches on the Island of Corfu. It is located 37 km away from the main Town. It has crystal clear seawater, an idyllic lush green landscape and stunning coves all of which makes this an ideal destination for your summer holiday. Despite its close proximity to the cosmopolitan holiday resort of Kassiopi, the beach has managed to keep a low profile. The small pebbled beach that lies around the crystalline bay offers some sun loungers and umbrellas with a perfect view of the Albanian coast. Kerasia beach is ideal for those who want to spend some time relaxing moments away from the noisy crowds and just sunbathe the day away…

The Best Beaches on Corfu:

Kontogialos Beach

Kontogialos beach is ideally located 13 km west of Corfu Town. The local area was a much preferred destination for the hippies during the 1960's. Today, in its present form it remains one of the most popular beaches on the Island of Corfu but now it is best known for its unique scenery and natural beauty. Kontogialos beach offers the visitor peaceful and relaxing moments by the sea. The beach consists of soft golden sand with an area of olive groves behind the middle section of beach that gives the visitor some welcome shade. The beach offers all the tourist facilities that visitors might want. There are good tavernas nearby that serve delicious Corfiot flavours and fine local wine. On Kontogialos beach there is plenty of water-sports available during the day such as water skiing and windsurfing for the more daring types…

The Best Beaches on Corfu:

Kouloura Village and Beach

Kouloura is a picturesque fishing village located 30 km south of Corfu Town and 7 km from the beautiful village of Kalami. The area is well known for its undulating areas of lush forests and the wonderful crystalline quality of its seawater. Kouloura beach is arguably one of the most attractive coves on the Ionian Island of Corfu because of its small pebbled beach and amazing scenery. The beach and bay area is well-sheltered creating a feeling of total privacy. Despite its small size, sunbeds cover the biggest part of the beach whereas trees are a nice alternative to relax under in the cool shade. At the right side of the beach is a picturesque port where several boats are always moored. This idyllic beach offers great swimming experiences and good sunbathing opportunities. There are tavernas within a short walk from the beach and the natural bay. It is an ideal destination for the visitors who seek a peaceful restful and relaxing holiday in a fabulous location…

The Best Beaches on Corfu:

Krouzeri Beach

Krouzeri beach is considered to be one of the most charming beaches on the Island of Corfu. It is located 25 km east of the main Town. The beach has been awarded with a Blue Flag for its cleanness and fine facilities. The beach consists of a mixture of white pebbles that blends perfectly with the golden sand that is lapped by the blue crystalline seawater. The sea is a kaleidoscope of blue colours that always amazes every visitor who comes to the beach. The beach also provides breathtaking sunset views and with the magnificent lush green scenery all around makes this an ideal destination which attracts lots of repeat visitors every summer. The natural beauty of Krouzeri beach provides the perfect ambiance for you to relax and enjoy the stunning scenery. The local area has many colourful flowers and olive groves. Krouzeri beach is the perfect place for a dreamy Greek Paradise holiday…

The Best Beaches on Corfu:

Limanaki Beach

Limanaki beach is a small beach that can be easily accessed within a very short walking distance from Corfu Town. In fact this lovely spot is located right beneath the Old Fortress. The seabed off the beach can be a bit uncomfortable, as it has a lot of small rocks, but the ambience of the place is nice and relaxing. The beach consists mainly of rock formations thus it is not recommended for children. Those adults who are interested in finding some privacy should definitely visit the beach although it has a lack of many of the basic tourist facilities…

The Best Beaches on Corfu:

Messonghi Beach

Messonghi is a small village located 22 km east of Corfu Town. It lies around a pristine beach, one of the most tranquil spots on the Island with good tourist facilities. The picturesque village of Messonghi is one of the oldest fishing villages on the Island of Corfu. Today the village is increasingly gaining in popularity as a quiet holiday destination. Off the beach you will find a wide range of tourist amenities and you will get a very warm welcome and good hospitality from the locals. Messonghi beach is always brimming with activity which is well spread out along the sweeping bay. The sight of stately olive groves and the undulating hills in the distance provide the perfect backdrop for a dream beach holiday tucked away from the din and bustle of some of the more touristy resorts. This beautiful beach is perfectly safe for swimming. Even children can indulge in a bit of swimming along the shorelines. The beach offers plenty of opportunities for water sports like jet skiing, speed boats but just as important it is a great bucket and spade beach too…

The Best Beaches on Corfu:

Paramonas Beach

Paramonas beach is located on the south west coast of the Island of Corfu, below the village of Agios Mattheos. The long beach is covered with soft golden sand and with some pebbles and large rocks on one side creating an imposing sight. The beach is fully equipped with sun beds and umbrellas. Paramonas beach is a good destination for nature lovers where the peaceful environment and the green landscape will captivate you the first time you see it. The lush green region offers a variety of day out choices, from nature hikes to having a family picnic on the beach or in the beautiful surrounding countryside…

The Best Beaches on Corfu:

Pelekas Beach

The picturesque Pelekas beach is ideally located 25 km west of Corfu Town. The beach is actually located on the bay directly opposite the main Town. The beach can be reached either by walking which shouldn't take more than 10 minutes or hiring a taxi that will speed you to this beach. Pelekas beach has been subjected to mass unrestricted tourism ever since the early 1960's and has ever since been a favourite destination for backpackers. The beach is of soft sand but sunbeds and umbrellas are not available here however, there are toilets and shower facilities provided. The beach is kept very clean. For those interested in going on a short excursion, a trip to the quaint fishing harbour to the south is likely to be a rewarding experience. For the intrepid thrill seekers, there are numerous rocky sea cliffs close by and from these you can experience some unique diving opportunities…

The Best Beaches on Corfu:

Perama Beach

Perama beach is located on the idyllic east coast of Corfu, 9 km from the main Town. It is surrounded by undulating hills that stand like a sentinel on the far horizon. For those interested it only takes a 10 minute drive from Corfu town, or you can even reach the beach on foot, it is a popular walking trail amidst lush green hills with perfect views of the many verdant coastal coves. Perama beach is ideal for all tastes. The biggest part of the sandy beach shore is covered with numerous sunbeds and umbrellas while on the side there is some free space for those who want some space to just sit directly onto the warm golden sand. There are a few bars and tavernas close by. It is from this beach that the renowned naturalist and conservationist Gerald Durrell first came across Corfu's rich marine underwater sea life. He uncovered several undiscovered aquatic species here. With this in mind and for the adventure lovers, Perama beach is ideal for indulging in an exciting session of snorkeling. The seawater here is crystal clear so one can easily enjoy the fascinating underwater landscape and see what strange underwater life you can spot lurking in the depths…

The Best Beaches on Corfu:

Pipitos Beach Kassiopi

Pipitos beach is close to the village of Kassiopi which is one of the largest villages on the Island of Corfu. It is located 36 km northeast of the main Town. We had a great summer holiday staying in this resort a few years ago and loved every moment of our stay. We explored many of the beaches featured in this book and enjoyed sunbathing and swimming on everyone. The main beach is quite popular with visitors and it is considered to be one of the most beautiful settings on the Island. Kassiopi has four main beaches, along with several smaller and less well known beaches, namely Kalamionas, Pipitos, Kanoni and Bataria. Pipitos beach is accessible primarily through a bout of rock climbing which makes it rather difficult to access for some. The beach largely offers sandy shores with rich green and cool blue crystalline seawater. Due to the absence of natural shade, umbrellas and sun beds are available on the beach. The beach has sand, shingles and pebbles which make walking comfortable, but plastic shoes or other beach foot wear is advised for children. For the more adventurous travellers there are large rock faces, waiting to be climbed close by. These magnificent rocks lead into the beautiful, deliciously cool seawater. Snorkeling, swimming and canoeing are a great joy here for those who are interested in enjoying these recreational activities…

The Best Beaches on Corfu:

Prasoudi Beach

Prasoudi beach is a marvellous beach located close to Agios Mattheos village. It is 27 km southwest of Corfu Town. It is a rather small sandy beach which is surrounded by lush green hills and olive trees. Prasoudi beach is pretty secluded and calm, great for some private moments away from the maddening crowds. It consists of sand and shallow clear seawater that make it an ideal swimming and sand castle building destination for families. Just above the beach, there is a taverna serving dishes of great Corfiot cuisine, wine and other welcoming ice cold drinks…

The Best Beaches on Corfu:

Roda Village and Beach

Below the mountain of Pantokrator lies the picturesque fishing settlement of Roda, just 20 km north of Corfu Town. Over the years, the village has grown in size offering plenty of modern amenities, restaurants, tavernas and lively music bars. This is a cosmopolitan village where tradition and modern life exist in perfect harmony. Roda is popular for its intense nightlife and for having a romantic atmosphere. The beautiful sandy beach and shore which is actually a natural continuation of the beach at Arachavi, stretches for a couple of km and has plenty of umbrellas and sunbeds provided. Various water sports facilities are also available. Those interested in short excursions to see more of the Island should visit the tourist resorts of Arachavi, Kassiopi and Sidari, located only a short distance from Roda village…

The Best Beaches on Corfu:

Rovinia Beach

Rovinia is a beautiful beach located in the wonderful scenic area of Paleokastritsa. It is located 20 km from the main Town of Corfu and it can be accessed by car or via a hiking path from the village of Liapades. Rovinia beach stands out for its unique natural beauty that attracts many visitors who just want to relax and view the stunning scenery. Tourist facilities would definitely disturb this unspoiled and tranquil environment as a result you will not find any, but the cave shaped rocks on the sides of the beach do offer some natural shade. Rovinia beach is a fabulous spot with blue green exotic seawater and a breathtaking rocky landscape with vast vegetation on top of it. The nature lovers amongst us will surely appreciate this green and pleasant paradise…

The Best Beaches on Corfu:

Santa Barbara Beach

Santa Barbara, or Marta, is one of the most popular beaches on Corfu located 40 km south of the main Town. The beach is set in a fabulous location surrounded by wild rocks and crystal clear seawater. There are tourist facilities available on the beach such as sunbeds and umbrellas for a large number of people. The seawater is very deep yet clean and safe. Despite its beautiful surroundings, there are no shady areas to be found close to the beach. Away from the beach a short walk will take you to a mini market and accommodation as well as tavernas and bars for food and cold drinks. The beach is easily accessed by car but parking is limited. It is often better to park on the roadside and walk down to the beach. Do not forget to take your bucket, spade and snorkel with you…

Mainland Greece

Our Holiday Voyage

Whilst on holiday on the Island of Corfu, one year, we went to the mainland of Greece, on a tour to explore the rich history and ancient sites of Classical Greece. Our ship left Corfu Town harbour and took us on our three day tour early one morning. The trip was led by an expert guide who was able to give us detailed information about all the places we were about to visit. We would, on the trip, be discovering the Delphi Archaeological Museum and sanctuary before then venturing over the Corinth Canal bridge to visit Epidaurus and finally travelling onto the City of Athens to visit all the ancient sites of the capital. In Athens we would be able to wonder around the city before visiting the acropolis with the majestic Parthenon standing proudly on its top. Once docked we started our journey of discovery by visiting Ancient Delphi…

Mainland Greece:

Delphi

Delphi is the second-most important archeological site in Greece (after the Acropolis in Athens). In ancient times Delphi was considered the place where heaven and earth met so the gods were very close-by here. Established around the 7th century BC, Delphi was a sanctuary to the god Apollo. It was here that the Oracle of Delphi was situated, the most trusted oracle in the ancient world from which the spirit of Apollo gave advice on everything from domestic matters to wars. Delphi had a theatre and many temples as well as the oracle. Today it has a well preserved stadium which once held chariot races. It was excavated from the mid-1800's and today the ruins stand impressively in their mountain landscape. Many believe that the place has a special magic and people have reported to being moved spiritually when they have visited Delphi. Ancient engravings on the stone at the site say such things as 'Know Thyself' and 'Nothing in Excess' could easily be from and inspired by today's self-help movement. Following our visit to Delphi it was back on the bus to head for the Corinth Canal…

Mainland Greece:

The Corinth Canal

The City of Corinth, which lies at the entrance to the Peloponnese region, conjoining as it does the Greek mainland and the Peloponnesian peninsula. The City was once a jewel of Greece in antiquity, and today it still remains one of Greece's most significant settlements boosting over 6,000 years of inhabited history. Although the City today is largely known as an industrial and administrative hub built in the early 20th-century, for the history buff, Corinth is the birthplace of many of the Greek myths and lore, and has many of its most important archeological sites and ruins,. Visiting here means you are immediately one step closer to the ancients. Just 4.3 miles away from the modern city are the ruins of ancient Corinth and Acrocorinth, where you can see elements of numerous eras, including the impressive medieval acropolis overlooking the ancient city. Modern Corinth doesn't shy to impress either, with the 3.9 miles long Corinth Canal, considered to be one of Greece's most important engineering achievements ever. The canal that cuts through the narrow Isthmus of Corinth and thus saving journeymen a 40 mile ride around the Peloponnese, this narrow canal is very impressive. As we boarded our bus and left Corinth behind and headed for the ancient site of Epidaurus…

Mainland Greece:

Epidaurus

Ancient Epidaurus in Greece is one of the most important archaeological sites of the country. It is famous for its Ancient Theatre that has amazing acoustics. The Ancient Theatre. Apart from the symmetry of this structure, the theatre is unique because of its excellent state of conservation. As already mentioned another distinctive detail about this construction is the perfect acoustics. In fact, if you drop a pin on the stage, it will be heard even if you are sitting in the very top seats of the theatre. In summer, this theatre hosts performances of ancient Greek drama. A few steps away from the Ancient Theatre is the Sanctuary of Asklepios, a very popular healing centre in antiquity. The nearby Archaeological Museum hosts many interesting exhibits from excavations made on this site. Most visitors go to Epidaurus Greece on a day trip tour from Athens. This is also a lovely region for people to holiday in so they can explore the many nice villages and beaches that can be found close to the ancient site, such as the seaside village of Ancient Epidaurus, a charming fishing village with a couple of small beaches, fish tavernas and several gift shops. Epidaurus is an area of mainland Greece located in the Peloponnese region. After our tour of the site it was back on the bus to go this time to the Greek capital City of Athens…

Mainland Greece:

The Athens Acropolis

We wandered around the city for a while before heading up to the Acropolis (Akropolis) which means "city on a hill" and dates from the 5th century BC. It is dominated by its main temple, the Parthenon, the Acropolis can be seen from all around the city of Athens. In 510 BC, the Delphic Oracle told Pericles that this hill should be a place to worship the gods, so he set about an ambitious building project which took half a century and employed both Athenians and foreign workers. It reflects the wealth and power of Greece at the height of its culture and influence. Notable structures within the Acropolis include the Temple of Athena Nike, the earliest fully Ionic temple on the site, built between 427 BC and 424 BC. Even now, the Classical architecture of the temples influences the building styles of our modern cities. But the thick pollution of Athens has taken its toll on the gleaming white marble of which the temples are made, as have souvenir-hunters, including the British Government, which still have the famous Elgin Marbles (a frieze from the Parthenon) in the British Museum. These days, the area is heavily protected and is undergoing massive restoration. It is a UNESCO World Heritage site…

Mainland Greece:

The Parthenon in Athens

The Parthenon (Parthenonas), is one of the world's most famous buildings. It represents a high point in ancient Greek architecture. Built around 440 BC, the Parthenon's classical architecture has influenced buildings ever since - and still does today. Built for worship of the goddess Athena, it was built to give thanks for the salvation of Athens and Greece in the Persian Wars. Officially it is called the Temple of Athena the Virgin; the name Parthenon comes from the Greek word for virgin. In the 2,500 years of its existence, the building has been a temple, a treasury, a fortress, and a mosque; in the 6th century AD the Parthenon became a Christian church, with the addition of an apse at the east end. Today The Parthenon is one of the world's leading tourist attractions. Built of Pentelic white marble, the Parthenon is famous for its classical Doric columns and decorating sculptural friezes which depict scenes of battle and history in marble. When it was built it was very colourful and was decorated in very bright colours indeed. Many of the friezes, known as the Elgin Marbles, are in the British Museum and there is fierce debate about whether they should be returned to Greece or not. As we leave this wonderful place and the politics behind after three very full days it was time to go back on board our ship and sail back to the Island of Corfu to continue our holiday in the sun, sand and sea. So now that we have explored all that the Island of Corfu has to offer and visited some of the famous ancient sites on the mainland of Greece it is now time, in the next chapter, to discover the culture and traditions of "**Being Greek**"…

Being Greek

Almost since time began Greece has been recognised as the birthplace of civilisation and democracy. Athens is one of the oldest cities in Europe. Greece and Athens in particular is also seen as the birthplace of democracy, Western philosophy, the Olympic Games, political science, Western literature, historiography, major mathematical principles, and Western theories of tragedy and comedy. Greece has given man its Gods of Mythology, the Olympic Games, The Parthenon, Minoan Culture and much, much more. In more recent times it has been the country of choice for a vast number of visitors (tourists) both to see its ancient cultural heritage sites, cities and to visit its multitude of paradise Islands. Greece has an abundance of fabulous beaches, rugged scenery and a warm, welcoming and friendly people…

Being Greek:

Alan and Susie on holiday in Greece

Susie and I have spent many a happy summer holiday on one or other of the many Greek Islands as well as being lucky enough to have been able to visit many of the important ancient sites and cities on the mainland of Greece over the last twenty years. During our holidays to Greece we have met and befriended many of the local people. We have, over the years, been told by our Greek hosts many interesting facts about Greece, its customs and its lovely people. We have found these facts very interesting and most enlightening. They explain many things about the Greeks and their ways that we did not know or even understand and so I have included these facts in the pages that follow so you too can begin to understand what it is "**Being Greek**"…

Being Greek:

Frappe Time…

Greece has an area of 50,949 square miles (131,958 square kilometres), Greece is roughly the size of Alabama. The population of Greece is more than 10 million people.

Greece attracts approximately 16.5 million tourists each year which is more than the country's entire population. Tourism constitutes nearly 16% of the Gross Domestic Product (GDP) of Greece.

In Greece everyone has to vote. Voting is required by law for every citizen who is 18 years of age or older.

About 7% of all the marble produced in the world comes from Greece.

Greece has more international airports than most other countries in the world. This is because so many foreign tourists want to visit its shores.

Greece is the world's third leading producer of olives, the Greeks have cultivated olive trees since ancient times. Some olive trees planted in the thirteenth century are still producing olives today…

Being Greek:

According to Greek mythology, Athena and Poseidon agreed that whoever gave the city of Athens the best gift would become guardian over the city. Though Poseidon gave the gift of water, Athena's gift of an olive tree was deemed by the other gods to be more valuable and so she became guardian of the city of Athens.

It is a fact that Greece has zero navigable rivers this is because of the mountainous terrain. Nearly 80% of Greece is mountainous.

In Greece approximately 98% of the people are ethnic Greeks. Turks form the largest minority group. Other minorities are Albanians, Macedonians, Bulgarians, Armenians, and gypsies.

About 12 million people around the world speak Greek. They live mostly in Greece, Cyprus, Italy, Albania, Turkey and the United States of America, among other countries.

Thousands of English words come from the Greek language, sometimes via the Roman adaptation into Latin and then into English. Common English words from Greek include "academy," "apology," "marathon," "siren," "alphabet," and "typhoon."…

Being Greek:

In the 1950's, only about 30% of Greek adults could read and write. Now, the literacy rate is more than 95%.

An old Greek legend says that when God created the world, he sifted all the soil onto the earth through a strainer. After every country had good soil, he tossed the stones left in the strainer over his shoulder and that is what created Greece.

Greece has more than 2,000 islands, of which approximately 170 are populated. Greece's largest island is Crete (3,189 sq. miles) (8,260 sq. km.).

Over 40% of the population of Greece lives in the capital Athens (*Athina* in Greek). Since becoming the capital of modern Greece, its population has risen from 10,000 in 1834 to 3.6 million in 2001.

Greece has had continuously inhabited for over 7,000 years.

The Greek civilization has been around for so long, that some would say, that it has had a chance to try nearly every form of government…

Being Greek:

Greece enjoys more than 250 days of sunshine each year which means that they have 3,000 hours of sun every year.

Currently, Greek men must serve from one year to 18 months in a branch of the counties armed forces. The government spends 6% of the annual Gross Domestic Product (GDP) on the military.

Ancient Greece was not a single country like modern Greece. Rather, it was made up of about 1,500 different city-states or *poleis* (singular, *polis*). Each had its own laws and army, and they often quarrelled and waged war on one another. Athens was the largest city-state.

Until the late 1990's, the greatest threat to Greece was Turkey, as the two nations have had historical disputes over Cyprus and other territory for decades. After coming to each other's aid after a devastating earthquake that hit both countries in 1999, their relationship has improved.

Currently the life expectancy for Greek females is 82 years and for men, 77 years. Greece is ranked 26th in the world for life expectancy rates.

Greece is the leading producer of sea sponges in the world…

Being Greek:

Football is the national sport of Greece.

Greek merchant ships make up 70% of the European Union's total merchant fleet. According to Greek law, 75% of a ship's crew must be Greek.

Greece has more archaeological museums than any other country in the world.

Retirement homes are rare in Greece. Grandparents usually live with their children's family until they die. Most young people live with their families until they marry.

Many Greek structures such as doors, windowsills, furniture, and church domes are painted a turquoise blue, especially in the Cyclades Islands. It is used because of an ancient belief that this shade of blue keeps evil away.

Feta cheese is made from goat's milk and is Greece's national cheese. It dates back to the Homeric ages, and the average per-capita consumption of feta cheese in Greece is the highest in the world…

Being Greek:

The Temple of Olympian Zeus in Athens

In Greece, people celebrate the "name day" of the saint that bears their name rather than their own birthday.

Thousands of birds stop in Greece's wetlands on their migrations. As many as 100,000 birds from northern Europe and Asia spend their winters there.

The saying "taking the bull by its horns" comes from the Greek myth of Hercules saving Crete from a raging bull by seizing its horns.

The city of Rhodes (the capital of the island of Rhodes) is famous for housing one of the Seven Wonders of the Ancient World: the Colossus of Rhodes (from which the word "colossal" is derived). This gigantic 98-foot (303-meter) statue of the god Helios, whose legs straddled the harbour, unfortunately was destroyed by an earthquake in 226 B.C.

The first Olympic Games took place in 776 B.C. The first Greek Olympic champion was a Greek cook named Coroebus who won the sprint race…

Being Greek:

Slaves made up between 40% and 80% of ancient Greece's population. Slaves were captives from wars, abandoned children, or children of slaves.

A long-standing dispute between Britain and Greece concerns the Elgin Marbles (the Greeks prefer to call them the Parthenon Marbles), which are housed in a London museum. The British government believes that it acquired them fairly through its purchase from Lord Elgin, while the Greeks claim the purchase was illegal as the marbles were the property of the Greek people and therefore, stolen.

Greece has one of the richest diversities of wildlife in Europe, including 116 species of mammals, 18 of amphibians, 59 of reptiles, 240 of bird, and 107 of fish. However, about half of the endemic mammal species are currently in danger of becoming extinct.

The monk seal has been a part of Greek's natural and cultural heritage and is described in **The Odyssey**. The head of a monk seal was even found on a coin dated back to 500 BC…

Being Greek:

Alexander the Great   Aristotle

Greece organized the first municipal rubbish/waste dump in the Western world around 500 B.C.

During the Nazi occupation of Greece in WWII, most Jews were taken to concentration camps across Europe. The Jewish population in Greece fell sharply from 78,000 to less than 13,000 by the end of the war.

In Greece, the dead are always buried because the Greek Orthodox Church forbids cremation. Five years after a burial, the body is exhumed and the bones are first washed with wine and then placed in an ossuary. This is done in part to relieve the shortage of land available in Greek cemeteries.

Government corruption cost Greece about $1 billion in 2009. Currently Greece's national debt is larger than the country's economy. Its credit rating, or its perceived ability to repay debts, is the lowest in the euro zone.

The Greek language has been spoken for more than 3,000 years, making it one of the oldest languages in Europe…

Being Greek:

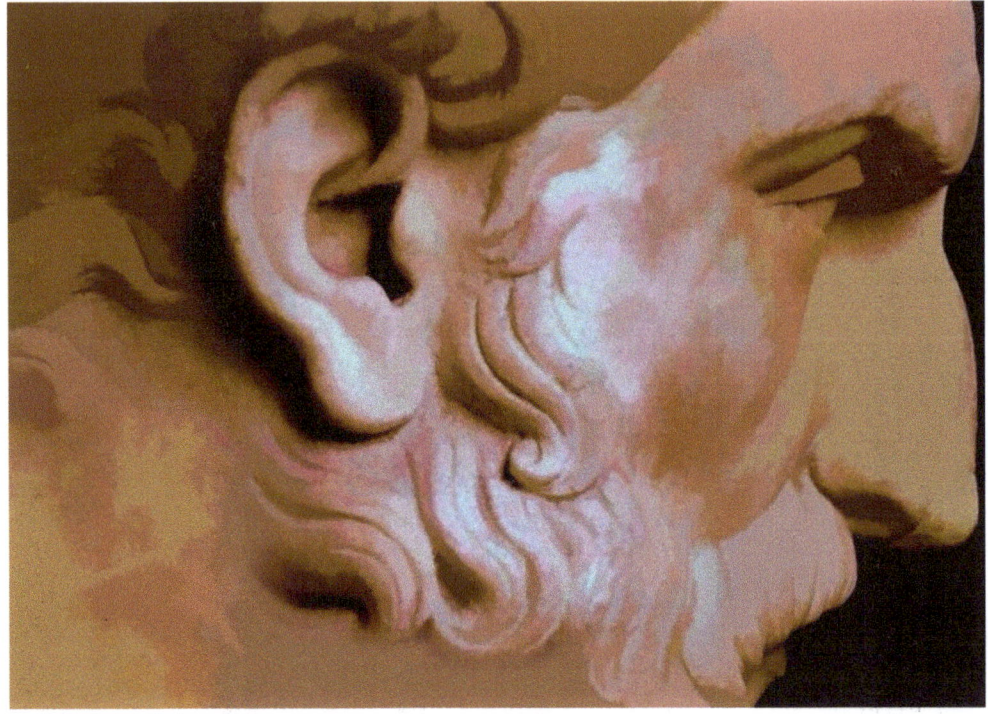

Epicurus

Greeks do not wave with an open hand. In fact, it is considered an insult to show the palm of the hand with the fingers extended. Greeks wave with the palm closed.

After giving a compliment, Greeks make a puff of breath through pursed lips, as if spitting. This is meant to protect the person receiving the compliment from the "evil eye".

No point in Greece is more than 85 miles (137 kilometres) from seawater. Greece has about 9,000 miles of coastline, the 10th longest coastline in the world.

Greece was once a mass of rock that was completely underwater. When a tectonic plate crashed into Europe, the collision raised the sea bed and created Greece's mountain ranges. The plate is still moving and causes earthquakes and tremors all around the Aegean.

Soldiers (*hoplites*) in ancient Greece wore up to 70 pounds (33 kilograms) of bronze armour…

Being Greek:

Socrates　　　　　　　　　　　　Plato

The first historian in the world is considered to be the Greek writer Herodotus (c. 484-425 B.C.), the author of the first great book of history on the Greco-Persian Wars.

The ancient Greeks are often called the inventors of mathematics because they were the first to make it a theoretical discipline. The work of Greek mathematicians such as Pythagoras, Euclid, Archimedes, and Apollonius lies at the basis of modern mathematics.

The first Greek philosopher is considered to be Thales of Miletus (c. 624-546 B.C.). He was the first to give a natural explanation of the origin of the world rather than a mythological one.

The Peloponnesian War (431-404 B.C.) between Athens and the Peloponnesian League led by Sparta left ancient Greece in ruins and marked the end of the golden age of Greece.

A Spartan specialty was a black soup made from salt, vinegar, and blood. No one in the rest of Greece would drink it…

Being Greek:

Greek Tragedy Masks

The British poet Lord Byron (1788-1824) was so enamoured with the Greeks that he travelled to Greece to fight against the Turks in the Greek War of Independence. He contracted a fever there and died at the age of 36. The Greeks consider him a national hero.

The word "barbarian" comes from Greek barbaroi, which means people who do not speak Greek and therefore sound like they're saying "bar-bar-bar-bar."

In ancient Greece one of the dishes enjoyed by ancient Greek men at feasts was roast pig stuffed with thrushes, ducks, eggs, and oysters. Most feasts were for men only, though there were female entertainers (this was not considered a respectable occupation for women).

The first Greek tragedy was performed in 534 B.C. and was staged by a priest of Dionysus named Thespis. He also wrote and performed a part separate from the traditional tragic chorus, which also designated him as the first actor. In fact, the word "thespian" (actor) derives from his name...

Being Greek:

The Spartans

At its height, Greek colonization reached as far as Russia and France to the west and Turkey to the Far East.

Pre-Socratic Greek philosopher Anaximander (c. 610-546 B.C.) is credited with writing the first philosophical treatise and making the first map of the known world. He can also be considered the first scientist who recorded a scientific experiment.

Spartan warriors (see above)were known for their long, flowing hair. Before a battle, they would carefully comb it. Cowardly soldiers would have half their hair and half their beards shaved off.

In ancient Greece wealthy people would sacrifice animals at the temples. Poor people who couldn't afford live animals offered pastry ones instead.

Ostracism allowed Athenian citizens to temporarily exile people who were thought dangerous to the public. If it was voted that ostracism was necessary, each citizen inscribed a name on a piece of pottery or ostracon in a secret ballet. The person with the most names had to leave town within 10 days for 10 years…

Being Greek:

Democritus   Heraclitus

Only boys and men were actors in ancient Greek plays. They wore large masks so audience members could see what part they were playing. Theatre staff carried big sticks to control the audience because sometimes the huge audiences would get excited by a play and would riot.

The term "Ancient Greece" usually refers to the time between Homer (750 B.C.) and the Roman conquest of Ptolemaic Egypt (Antony and Cleopatra, 30 B.C.).

Democracy in Athens was significantly different from modern democracies in that it was both more participatory and exclusive. There were also no political parties in Athenian democracy.

The Greeks, in ancient times, would sacrifice one hundred bulls to the God Zeus during each Olympic Games.

The Greeks revolutionized the art of sculpture. Instead of stiff poses and blank faces, Greek artists began to carve statues of people that showed both movement and emotion…

Being Greek:

Bringing in the Harvest Greek style

The Greek Temple of Artemis, built on the site of two earlier shrines dating back as far as the eight century B.C. in modern-day Turkey, was one of the Seven Wonders of the Ancient World. It was built around 550 B.C. and was destroyed in 356 B.C. by Herostratus.

The Parthenon (Place of the Partheons, from parthenos or "virgin") was built almost 2,500 years ago and sits on the Acropolis above the city of Athens. It actually featured colourful sculptures and a large gold-and-ivory statue of Athena. It took 15 years to build.

The ancestors of the Greeks were Indo-Europeans who entered Greece around 1900 B.C. They lived alongside the Minoans for many centuries before giving rise to the Mycenaean civilization which ended abruptly in the twelfth century B.C. After a "dark ages" of 300 years in which the knowledge of writing was lost, Greece gave birth to one of the most influential civilization the world has ever known: Classical Greece.

By law, the only people eligible for citizenship in Sparta were direct descendants of the original Doric settlers. Because of this, there were never more than about 6,000-7,000 male citizens in Sparta, compared with up to 40,000 in Athens...

Being Greek:

Greek Masks…

Greek's highest elevation is the legendary home of Zeus and other Olympian gods and goddesses, Mount Olympus at 9,750 feet (2,917 meters). Its lowest elevation is the Mediterranean Sea, or sea level.

Alexander the Great was the first Greek ruler to put his own face on Greek coins. Previously, Greek coins had shown the face of a god or goddess.

The word "tragedy" is Greek for "goat-song" because early Greek tragedies honoured Dionysus, the god of wine, and the players wore goatskins. Tragedies were noble stories of gods, kings, and heroes. Comedy or "revel," on the other hand, were about lower-class characters and their antics.

The most famous modern writer in Greece is Nikos Kazantzakis (1883-1957). His novels **Zorba the Greek** and **The Last Temptation of Christ** were both made into movies.

Greece's official name is the Hellenic Republic. It is also known as Ellas or Ellada…

Being Greek:

The Greek flag includes nine blue-and-white horizontal stripes, which some scholars say stand for the nine syllables of the Greek motto "Eleftheria i Thanatos" or "Freedom or Death." Blue represents Greece's sea and sky, while white stands for the purity of the struggle of freedom. In the upper left-hand corner is the traditional Greek Orthodox cross.

Greece has two major political parties: the Socialists (Panhellenic Socialists Movements or PASOK) and the Democrats (the New Democracy Party). Both were founded in 1974 after Greece's military dictatorship collapsed.

Greece has one of the lowest divorce rates in the EU. Greece traditionally also has the highest abortion rates.

About 10% of a Greek worker's pay is taken for taxes and another 10% for national health care in return the government provides free hospitals and other medical services.

Greek workers currently get at least one month off paid vacation every year…

Being Greek:

A Roman Soldier

About 10% of Greek adults are unemployed. Even with a college education, it's hard to find a job in Greece today.

Greece's previous currency, the drachma, was 2,650 years old and Europe's oldest currency. The drachma was replaced with the Euro in 2002.

Throughout history, Greeks have loved the sea. They have more than 1,800 merchant ships in service currently. Greece has one of the largest merchant shipping fleets in the world. Aristotle Onassis and Stavros Niarchos ("The Golden Greek") are some of the best-known Greek shipping businessmen.

When the Roman Empire split in two in A.D. 285, the eastern half, including Greece, became known as the Byzantine Empire. In 1453, Greece fell to the Ottoman Empire. Greece wouldn't achieve independence until 1829.

Greece is the European country with the largest number of newspapers. There are 18 daily newspapers in Athens. Foreign papers can also be found in large cities and on popular holiday Islands…

Being Greek:

Roadside Shrine…

The Electricity supply in Greece is 220 volts AC, 50Hz. Round two-pin plugs are used. North American visitors require a transformer and British visitors an adaptor.

The time in Greece is like most other counties in Europe, Summer (Daylight-Saving) Time is observed in Greece, where the time is shifted forward by 1 hour; 3 hours ahead of Greenwich Mean Time (GMT+3). After the summer months the time in Greece is shifted back by 1 hour to Eastern European Time (EET) or (GMT+2).

In Greece the working hours for Banks and Public Services work are from 08.00 to 14.00, Monday to Friday. The shops are usually open Monday-Wednesday-Saturday from 09.00 to 15.00 and Tuesday-Thursday-Friday from 09.00 to 14.00 and 17.00 to 20.00. In these three days of the week, shops close for the siesta at noon and open again in the afternoon. In the tourist areas in high season, most shops stay open all day long, from early in the morning till late in the evening. Malls in the cities also stay open all day.

Anyone who has visited Greece will be well aware of the numerous small roadside shrines that often contain lit candles and vases of dried flowers. These are erected at sites where loved ones have had a tragic, often fatal, accident and their family leave them a light to remember them…

Being Greek:

Driving in Greece: For those of you that have already sampled the delights of driving on Greek roads you will be familiar with the sometimes unfinished state of the road surface and of the sides of the road and ditches being full of builder's rubble and litter. Beside many of the main roads you will see large advertising boards touting brands of cigarettes, coffee and/or sporting goods.

Greek time: In the summertime, Greece is two hours ahead of the time in the UK (Greenwich meridian time) like elsewhere in Europe. Also in Greece, in the summer season (March – September) you will find that there is something very curious about time. In Greece it is conceived in a very particular way. Here time is not running, there is no such concept of "being on time or late" and a watch is just something to wear. The Greeks themselves are aware of the need for them to take it easy (but not in serving the tourist!) up to the point that G.M.T. is not considered as the Greenwich Meridian Time, but as the Greek Maybe Time! So remember you are on holiday take your time and relax things will get done in the fullness of time or should I say in Greek time.

Religious festivals: Throughout Greece, religious festivals have become a true backbone to many communities. All kinds of festivals and religious feast events take place for example Christian Holy events during Easter, when churches are covered with colourful flowers and bay leaves…

Being Greek:

The rosary that most of the Greek men are holding in their hands, sitting outside the kafeneion (cafe in Greece), has no religious meaning, but is only a way of killing time. Try and buy one, it's actually much more difficult to swing it than it looks.

The iron bars sticking out from the flat Greek house roof are exclusively there for the purpose of a later extension to the house. They have **NOTHING** to do with exemptions from taxpaying, as long as the house isn't yet finished. (It is a good story though)!

On an Olive tree the fact that the trunks of the trees are often painted white (lime-wash) in Greece it is used primarily to fight ants. And besides it looks nice, too!

A single person sitting at a taverna, can wait quite a long time for the waiter to show up. In Greece it's very unlikely that anybody eats alone. He/she must be waiting for someone. For the waiter it will be very impolite and bumptious, to ask for the order before all the guests have arrived. This has changed in the major tourist places, and especially for tourists, but you can run into this phenomenon in the villages of many places in Greece…

Being Greek:

When the Greeks go out for dinner, they always pay cash. NO cheque's and credit cards! And they have always got money enough to pay the bill for their company too. Not being able to pay, would be humiliating beyond belief.

Unfinished buildings is a common sight in Greece. The reason is that Greek people build what they need today and leave the rest of the building unfinished for the future. It may seem that the Greeks are constantly building houses - and they are. Most Greek parents build a house for each daughter, but not for their sons (as they are supposed to marry a girl who will get a house from her parents). Often it is also the daughter that inherits her parents' or grandparents' house when they die.

You might get the impression that Greek men always sit in cafes and drink. They do often go to a kafeneion, but not always, and rarely for a very long time. Often they have a cup of Greek coffee only. Most of them stay there for a short time, just enough to hear what has happened and also to make an appointment with for example the local electrician or the local bricklayer. Of course, Greek women can go to the kafeneion as well, but most of them don't want to, and besides they hear all the gossip from the husband when he comes home. For about 20 years ago, you would always find at least two kafenions in a village, no matter how small it was, but painted in different colours. The colours indicated the political party of the owner of the kafenion. This way you avoided political quarrels. Rather practical! It can still be found, but it has become more and more rare as less and less people care about politics in Greece…

Being Greek:

Theft is very, very rare in Greece. It's simply considered too humiliating to steel other people's things or money. On the other hand it's OK to cheat a bit - especially if they don't like the person they cheat.

You will see a Greek priest - or pappas, as they are called - everywhere, as you cannot miss them in their long, black dress and high hat. They are not obliged to wear their priest clothes all the time, but they do, as it is most practical and they are easier to identify this way.

Greek priests can marry and have children, just like in the Lutheran church. But you will never see a woman priest. This is not allowed by the Greek Orthodox Church.

At most beaches you will have to pay for a sun bed and an umbrella. If you think that it is just people trying to get money out of the tourists you're very wrong. It's a job in Greece having a piece of a beach. A man bids for a particular part of the beach each year, and he pays a sum of money, to be allowed to put up his sun beds and umbrellas. During the season it is his responsibility that this part of the beach is kept properly. The price you pay will depend on where the beach is situated, what kind of facilities (taverna, toilets, showers) there are. The tourist police checks that he does his job properly…

Being Greek:

If you want to see a Greek Church or monastery inside, you must be properly dressed. It's considered rude to enter a church if your shoulders and knees aren't covered. This rule goes for both men and women. So if you are a tourist and wants to be polite in the country you are visiting then please dress respectfully when visiting a church.

If a Greek invites you out for dinner or a drink, don't **EVER** try to make him "split the bill in half" as we often do here in Northern Europe. I know some tourists who have wanted to be nice to their host for the evening, and they snapped the bill out of his hand and paid it. Never has a friendship been that close to ruin, and the Greek man was more embarrassed than you could ever imagine!

If you are invited to a Greek home, remember to bring something for the hosts. Flowers or chocolate is the most common. If the occasion is a name day, you must bring a present, which you deliver when you enter the house. The present will be put together with the rest of the presents on a table - unopened. The Greeks will open the gifts when all the guests have left. If he or she doesn't like the gift they don't have to pretend and show a lot of gratitude that they really do not feel. Actually it is a very practical habit.

Officially there is equality between the sexes, but still in Greece today women are paid less…

Being Greek:

About 40 % of the Greek women are engaged in active employment.

Theoretically Greek women are liable for military service, but only volunteers are taking part in the service, and the women seem to be satisfied with this situation.

When divorcing, all belongings are equally split between the man and woman.

Today a Greek woman may keep her maiden name when marrying.

Today Greek women only give birth to half as many children, as they did before World War 2. The birth-rate is the second lowest in Europe. Italy has the lowest birth-rate.

Since 1982 it has been legal to have a civil marriage. But still 95 % are married religiously in the church.

Arranged marriages are forbidden by law. Paying dowry is illegal too. But still you can see examples of both especially in the remote villages…

Being Greek:

The average age for Greek women is 82 years. Men live usually until 77 years of age.

Bullet holes in road signs. It is no secret that Greeks own guns, especially in mountainous areas. Road signs are easy targets and you will see many of them that resemble Swiss cheese after suffering some shooting practice. Greeks also usually fire their guns at weddings and other celebrations.

Churches (ekklisies): Big churches are usually found inside the towns but the numerous small ones are practically everywhere. Usually they are white-painted, you will find them on a beach, on the mountain peaks, in deep gorges or inside caves. The people of Greece are deeply religious people and they build churches to express their gratitude to God or to fulfil a "tama", a promise given to God in exchange for a request. The miniature churches next to the roads however, are memorials for people killed in a car accident, at the same spot where the accident happened. The family of the deceased construct and maintain them. They contain a photo of the deceased, some religious objects and a lit candle.

Erotas or Eros, son of Aphrodite, was a god in ancient Greece: It is difficult to give the meaning of the Greek word "erotas" because there is no word for it in English. The closest translation is "being in love". The English word Love is "Agapi" in Greek…

Being Greek:

Erontas or diktamos is the Greek name for the herb dittany: It used to be a rare, hard to collect herb because it grew on steep cliffs in mountainous areas. Today it is cultivated, so it has become easy to find. It is said that its name "erontas", which is actually the same word as erotas, was given to it because a man should be deeply in love with a woman in order to risk his life to collect it for her from a steep cliff.

Fresh fish in Greece has become rare and quite expensive. Common fish that you will find at restaurants are: red mullet, sea bream, red snapper, swordfish and tuna. Octopus, squids, shrimps and mussels are also easy to find and they taste great. Fish like Sand-Smelt or Silverside are quite cheap and tasty, although its taste is described as "fishy" by people who are not used to Mediterranean fish.

Garides are shrimps: Have them boiled or "saganaki" with tomatoes and feta cheese…

Being Greek:

A Greek Salad: In Greek it is called "horiatiki" and it is a tasty salad made from fresh tomatoes, cucumber, olives and feta cheese. Add some oregano, vinegar and plenty of Greek olive oil and you have a tasty and fulfilling dish.

Herbs: If I had to describe Greece in just five words only, then I would choose: sun, sea, mountains, sage and thyme. Sage and thyme are everywhere in Greece and the air is full of their characteristic smell. Herbs have been used for ages by people of Greece as medicines. Try a tea of camomile and sage if you have a sore throat. If you do not like the taste you can add some honey to it. If your nose is blocked and you cannot breathe easily, then have a tea made from thyme.

Honey of excellent quality is produced in Greece. Thyme honey is considered to be the best.

Immigrants: Albanians, Bulgarians, Russians, Ukranian and others from Eastern Europe have moved to Greece in big numbers. Most of them work in agriculture and construction and their number is more than 10% of the Greek population. They adjusted quickly to the Greek way of life and their children go to Greek schools…

Being Greek:

Kafeneio, the Greek café: Is a very important part of the social life of all parts of Greece. They often say that you should always find the time for a coffee.

Lamb meat: The best meat you can have in Greece is the young lamb or young goat meat from animals raised in the mountainous areas. If you happen to be in a taverna in a small mountainous village, ask them for grilled paidakia.

Mizithra: A fresh soft white cheese. It contains lower fat and cholesterol than yellow cheese. It is made from sheep's milk.

Paximadi: The traditional Greek way of preserving bread for a long time. It is hard dried bread that gets soft when you add some water to it. You will find it in various forms, sizes and made from wheat or barley, with or without yeast, whole grain or not. Pour some olive oil on a big round piece of paximadi, add some grated tomato, oregano and feta cheese and you will have the very tasty appetizer.

Pita Giros are slices of grilled pork meat with yoghurt, lots of onion, French fries, salt and pepper, all wrapped inside a round "pita" bread. Pita - giros is the fast food of Greece and you can find it almost everywhere. Chicken giros is becoming popular lately because of the smaller amount of fat that it contains…

Being Greek:

Platanos or Plane Tree: A tree that grows close to water. You can find it usually close to a river in gorges or in the central square of villages in Greece. It looks similar to the maple tree and it can grow very big.

Souvlaki is skewered pork meat, a traditional Greek dish. It is served with French fries and there is also chicken, lamb and swordfish souvlaki…

Being Greek:

Greece produces many different vegetables and they taste a lot better than what you will find in the supermarkets in the rest of Europe.

Xanthies: blonde tourist women. Highly appreciated by the "kamakia", the young hot-blooded Greek lovers. Love stories between men of Greece and tourists are common each year. Most of them are just summer love but a few marriages come out of them. The result is that there are many European women living in Greece, mostly German, Dutch and Scandinavian. Be aware though, that having a romantic love affair during your holiday is one thing and living in Greece married to a Greek man is totally different. The cultural differences are many and it is very important not to ignore them.

Zucchini or Courgette. Try zucchini slices deep fried in olive oil. Fried aubergine slices are very tasty too.

Yannis and Yorgos, are the two most common names for men in Greece. Yannis is John and Yorgos is George. More common names are Manolis and Nikos. For women the most common name is Maria.

Now that we understand a bit more about the Island of Corfu, the Greek mainland and what it is like **"Being Greek"** it is time for us to say goodbye, so until the next time, keep well, be happy and I hope you have enjoyed our time together…

Acknowledgement

I would like to thank all the people of the Island of Corfu all their kindness and helpfulness during our many holidays to this lovely Island. Susie and I both look forward to hopefully seeing them all again very soon.

I would also like to thank my publishers Rainbow Publications UK. For publishing this book and for giving me the opportunity for my words to be read once more. Finally I wish to thank my wife Susie for her love, help and support that she gives me in all that I do every day of my life.

Susie… …Alan

Copyright © 2019 Alan R. Massen

I wish you all a very big

Thank You…

www.ingramcontent.com/pod-product-compliance
Lightning Source LLC
Chambersburg PA
CBHW061926290426
44113CB00024B/2829